Four-stroke
Handbook

Four-stroke Handbook

The new alternative in model engines

Bill Burkinshaw

ARGUS BOOKS

Argus Books Limited
1 Golden Square
London W1R 3AB
England

ISBN 0 85242 879 0

Phototypesetting by En to En, Tunbridge Wells
Printed and bound by The Garden City Press,
Pixmore Avenue, Letchworth, Herts. SG6 1JS

Contents

Chapter 1	Four-stroke engines	6
Chapter 2	Valves and lubrication	18
Chapter 3	Practical considerations	30
Chapter 4	Mountings and fuel supply	44
Chapter 5	Starting and running	56
Chapter 6	Fuels and plugs	66
Chapter 7	Servicing	78
Chapter 8	Increasing power	87
Appendix 1	Four-strokes by capacity	96
Appendix 2	Major engine dimensions	112

1 Four-stroke engines

Since the mid 1970s the Four Stroke model engine has steadily grown in popularity in the world of R/C model aircraft, consistently gaining ground over its still numerically dominant cousin, the Two Stroke. The earliest commercially manufactured four-strokes were greeted with some scepticism, it being felt that they were little more than curiosities destined to find places in the showcases of engine collectors but of little practical use to serious modellers. Just how wrong these early feelings were can be judged on virtually every model flying site up and down the country where the virtues of the modern four-stroke are now being appreciated.

Four-stroke motors are not a new phenomenon to model aircraft. As far back as 1914 D. Stanger established a world record of 51 seconds flying a V4 configuration four-stroke powered free-flight biplane. Nearly thirty years later, the American 'Feeney' four-stroke became the first such engine to be commercially available in any quantity. The Feeney was available in three capacities, 20, 15 and 10 cc, known as Models A, B and C respectively. It had a poor reputation for both constructional quality and performance and never really competed with the popular two-strokes of the time. Co-designer of the Feeney, Casimir Leja, went on to design a further spark ignition engine which was advertised in the late 1940s.

Falling in between the advents of the Leja-inspired designs was the Morton M-5 radial, a 5 cylinder overhead valve radial engine which was made, sold and used in fair numbers right up to the mid 1950s. Closer to home, the Channel Islands to be specific, the 'Channel Islands Special' was being produced in commercial quantities but sales were disappointing, the market not being really ready for four-strokes. Examples are now keenly sought, some still being seen regularly at Vintage modelling meetings. The C.I. Special was a very practical 10 cc (0.60 cu.in) capacity spark ignition engine with a clever positive feed lubrication system for the crankcase. A year or two later the much-loved 'Gannet' four-stroke of 15 cc (0.90 cu.in.) capacity first appeared; few air-cooled versions were built, but the

6

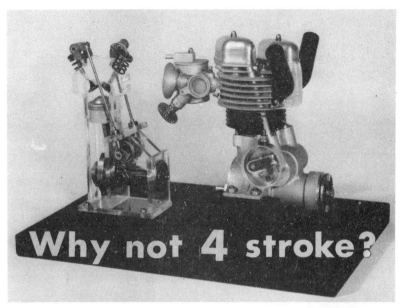

The heading of Professor Chaddock's article in January 1966 *Aeromodeller*, believed to be the starting point for modern four-stroke engine development.

standard water-cooled marine engine still powers a fair number of model boats.

In spite of the proven practicality of the four-stroke a gap of more than ten years separated the demise of the C.I. Special from the next step on the route of progress, which came in the form of a thought-provoking article in *Aeromodeller* magazine of January 1966 from the pen of Professor Dennis Chaddock, who backed up his theoretical discourse with photographs and performance details of a very modern looking four-stroke single.

Some years later, at the Model Engineer Exhibition held in London, Mr Ogawa, the President of one of the major Japanese engine manufacturers, OS, met and talked at length with Professor Chaddock. We can only surmise what the subjects of discussion were, but it is a fair assumption that Ogawa already knew of Professor Chaddock and his design work in the fields of both two- and four-stroke engines and had also seen his article of some years before. What is a matter of fact is that the first OS four-stroke engine appeared in first prototype and then production form within a comparatively short span of time following the meeting.

Once an engine from a manufacturer of the status enjoyed by OS was in the arena it became only a matter of time before other

7

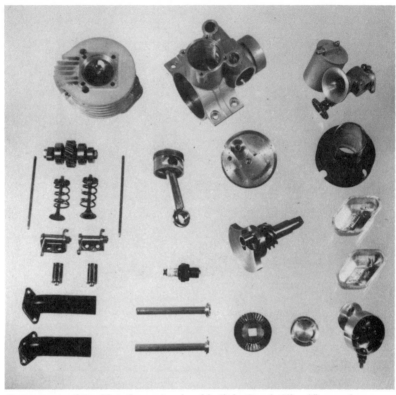

Components of the *Matador* engine, hand-built by Derek Giles. The crankcase and cylinder head are machined from solid forged duralumin – no castings were used anywhere in the engine.

manufacturers felt obliged to follow and the fashion-conscious modeller felt compelled to purchase.

Why four-strokes?

To understand the reasons for the acceptance of these motors so rapidly in the late 1970s compared with the lack of general interest that earlier launches of four-strokes met, it is necessary to appreciate the still current situation in which many R/C modellers find themselves with regard to the non-modelling public. Whether modellers like it or not, to many people their models are anti-social – they are noisy. A continual quest for additional power from the established two-stroke forced engine designers along the path of rising engine revolutions per minute (RPM) with a consequent rise in noise levels both from exhaust and propeller. Lack of real willingness on the part of modellers to accept that the solution of larger more efficient silencers fitted to their models could minimise the problem started to result in loss of flying sites. Manufacturers of engines were similarly loth to embark on programmes of development of quieter silencers for fear of ending up with a range of quiet but potentially lower power engines with limited sales appeal. The 'add-on' silencer enjoyed a brief period of popularity but was really not the most effective way of dealing with the problem.

The power chase was probably only of limited interest to the majority of modellers, but they were caught up in the spiral, since only high power, noisy motors seemed to be being developed. The possibility of purchasing a new form of engine of modest but practical power output that would not produce the anti-social exhaust note so hated by the environmentally conscious was seized upon. Couple the low noise factor with the appeal of a superb piece of precision engineering, the initial novelty value, low fuel consumption plus the kudos of owning something that was certain to draw attention, not to mention the exclusivity value granted by virtue of price, and the scene was set for a boom in sales as the Far Eastern manufacturers raced into production.

By a happy coincidence, a blossoming interest in 'Vintage' style models coincided with the advent of the four-stroke. Although the idea of powering model designs of the 30s, 40s and 50s with the absolute latest in model engine technology seems in itself a contradiction, the nature of the four-stroke is such that its relaxed, quiet, low-revving power seems somehow in sympathy with the aura of the Vintage model, producing a relaxing form of sports aircraft that a growing number of modellers have become addicted to.

Nor have scale modellers been slow to embrace the four-stroke. The incongruity of a scale model aircraft endeavouring to

The Channel Island Special was a fine engine but ahead of its time. Even at £7.50 it failed to find a market in 1949.

The Morton M5 five-cylinder radial was produced about 40 years ago. Its attractive appearance but short running life made it most suitable for collectors.

replicate the flight performance of its full-sized counterpart while accompanied by a high-pitched two-stroke exhaust note had long frustrated the scale purists. It was practical to quieten the exhaust note, albeit often at the expense of an overheating engine, but try as they did it was not possible to disguise the pitch of the note, unrealistic by anyone's standards. The lower operating RPM of the four-stroke and its comparatively high torque level enabled larger propellers than hitherto thought possible to be turned efficiently, producing flying performances that confounded many doubters, with accompanying deeper, more realistic exhaust notes. Indeed,

Four-strokes lend themselves to many scale designs, especially exposed-cylinder Fairchild and similar models. Dummy cylinders or multi-cylinder engines retain general scale appearance.

quite a few models of light aircraft could now fly using scale diameter propellers, some even with the pitch being correct if they were models of full-sized craft with anti-clockwise rotating motors.

Two-stroke and four-stroke cycles

It is my contention that to get the best from your engine it is of benefit to understand what makes it tick! Firstly, a brief explanation of the simpler two-stroke.

The invention of the two-stroke cycle is attributed to a gentleman called Otto. Let us be quite clear at this point: the various operations that follow one another to produce power from both two-stroke and four-stroke engines are correctly known as a 'cycle'. There is only one 'cycle' of operation in either type of engine. In the simpler engine: which has only three moving parts (piston, connecting rod and crankshaft) there are two strokes to each cycle, but in the engine type that forms the subject matter of this book there are four strokes to each cycle. The two-stroke cycle is as follows:

Figure 1 Two-stroke cycle.

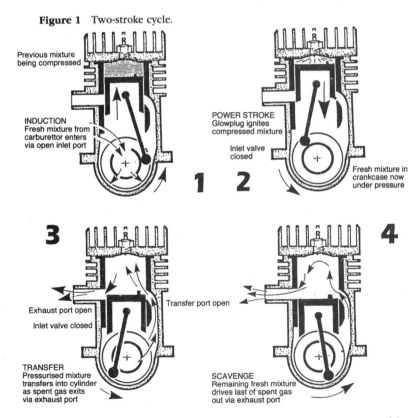

Previous mixture being compressed

INDUCTION
Fresh mixture from carburettor enters via open inlet port

POWER STROKE
Glowplug ignites compressed mixture

Inlet valve closed

Fresh mixture in crankcase now under pressure

1 2

3

Exhaust port open

Inlet valve closed

Transfer port open

TRANSFER
Pressurised mixture transfers into cylinder as spent gas exits via exhaust port

4

SCAVENGE
Remaining fresh mixture drives last of spent gas out via exhaust port

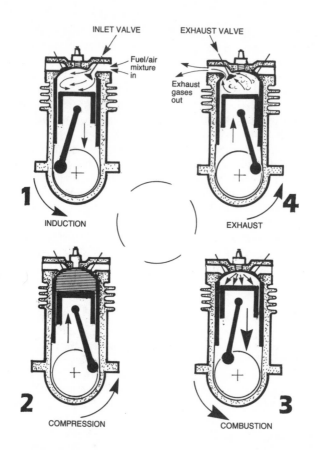

Fig. 2
Four-stroke
cycle.

(a) Piston 'Up' stroke 1 – fuel and air is mixed in the carburettor to form a gas which is drawn into the sealed crankcase of the engine.

(b) Piston 'Down' stroke 1 – gases in the crankcase are compressed and driven into the combustion chamber via transfer passages.

(c) The next time the piston goes 'Up' there is a combustible gas in the combustion chamber which is first compressed then ignited at a suitable point. This ignition can be by a spark, heat of compression (the Diesel principle), or a Glow Plug (the Semi-Diesel).

(d) Simultaneously the rising piston causes the fuel/air gas mixture for the next cycle to be drawn into the crankcase.

(e) The burning fuel expands and drives the piston down with a simultaneous compressing of the crankcase gases then opening the exhaust port and expelling the combustion by-products through the exhaust port ready for the transfer phase.

The whole operation is now continuous, the two strokes being generally described as – Stroke 1, Induction and Compression; Stroke 2, Combustion and Exhaust. See Figure 1.

The four-stroke cycle is more complex, however, since instead of the piston controlling the inlet, exhaust and transfer of gases, a system of valves does the job. The classic four-stroke motor has two valves per cylinder, one to admit fresh fuel/air mixture, known as the Inlet Valve, the other controlling the exhausting of the burnt gases, the Exhaust Valve. These two valves are opened and closed by a pair of Cams driven at half crankshaft speed by gears from the crankshaft. Each valve therefore opens and closes once during the four strokes of the cycles as follows:

(a) The piston descends and the inlet valve opens to admit the fuel/air mixture from the carburettor. As the piston reaches the bottom of its stroke the inlet valve closes.
(b) The piston rises back up the cylinder, compressing the fuel/air mixture which is ignited either by spark, glow-plug or pure heat of compression (Diesel principle again).
(c) The burning and expanding gases drive the piston down the cylinder applying a force to the crankshaft via the connecting rod. As the piston descends, the exhaust valve starts to open.
(d) The piston moves back up the cylinder, driving the burnt fuel residues out of the cylinder, purging it of pollutants prior to the whole cycle starting over again. See Figure 2.

The areas of advantage of the four-stroke over the simpler two-stroke can be summarised under three headings.

Low noise level

Engine noise comes from several sources: exhaust, inlet, mechanical noise and propeller noise. Additionally, vibration produced by the engine generates further airframe noise as the model acts as a sounding board.

First thoughts on the exhaust noise of a four-stroke would lead one to suppose that the exhaust noise would be halved. This is not strictly true, as the valve timing of the engine has a marked effect on the exhaust noise. The earlier the exhaust valve opens during the exhaust stroke, the higher will be the pressure in the cylinder and the higher the velocity of the escaping gases. Since performance of four-strokes is largely governed by the timing of the valves there is a tendency to advance the opening of the exhaust valves to improve power output, with a corresponding high level of noise from each individual power stroke. Of course, there are only half the power strokes for any particular RPM that there would be for a two-stroke motor, so the noise level is reduced and RPM tend to be lower anyway.

The same can be said for inlet noise. The rush of air into the cylinder through the carburettor is a much more restrained affair than in the two-stroke and noise generated is thus lower. Propeller noise should never be forgotten: anyone who has heard a high-power electric motor running with a propeller attached will realise that propellers do generate considerable noise. Lower operating RPM do give the four-stroke a noise advantage here as well, particularly as the stiffer wooden and glass-filled nylon propellers that are a must for four-stroke operation are inherently quieter than flexible nylon types anyway.

Airframe noise is a difficult area. It is often noted that four-strokes tend to vibrate more heavily than two-strokes, but if the vibration transmitted to the airframe is of greater intensity it is of lower frequency, so on balance there is almost certainly a benefit in this area.

If engines up to 0.61 cu.in. capacity are considered, then virtually without exception, even with the most rudimentary of silencers the four-stroke will be a quieter proposition than a two-stroke of equivalent size. However, over 0.61 cu.in. capacity the situation does start to change. There is no doubt that the larger engines do need silencers to bring them down to acceptable levels of noise output. It is fair to say that the silencer required will not be anything like as large as that required for a two-stroke of the same capacity, as after all, there is theoretically only half the volume of gas to contend with at any given RPM.

Propeller noise must start to play a very significant part in noise generation on larger engines because of greater area and higher tip speed, and such things as small nicks and poor surface finish on very large propellers of 16 inch diameter and upwards will also make a noticeable difference to the noise developed.

With the reservations outlined above, it can be stated that the four-stroke is a quieter engine than the two-stroke.

Fuel consumption

Thanks to the precision with which the operating cycle of the four-stroke can be controlled by cam design and the benefit obtained by the positive exhaust stroke of the cycle driving virtually all the burnt gases from the combustion chamber, the four-stroke is able to burn the fuel it draws into the cylinder very much more efficiently than the two-stroke. The major disadvantage of the two-stroke from the

14

A clear advantage of four-strokes is that often propeller size can be very close to scale, as is obvious on this splendid D.H. 86 *Dragon*.

point of view of efficiency is the poor 'scavenging'of the cylinder. As there is a degree of overlap between the phases of the operating cycle it is characteristic that there will be exhaust residues left in the cylinder as the 'fresh' charge of fuel/air mixture is transferred to the combustion chamber. This pollution of the fuel reduces the efficiency and attempts to overcome this by opening the transfer and exhaust ports earlier in the cycle so that the exhaust is driven out by the incoming fresh fuel/air mixture results in a further reduction of efficiency, as a proportion of the fresh gas goes straight out through the exhaust port.

There is a degree of overlap between phases of operation of the four-stroke, but broadly speaking the cylinder is charged with truly fresh mixture for each cycle and little goes out through the exhaust port. Also as a result of the fine degree of control over timing of the cycle of operation, it is possible firstly to compress the mixture more efficiently, allow it to expand more fully during the power stroke and generally use a higher average cylinder pressure than is commonly found in the two-stroke. Efficiency may not sound altogether too important to the model flier but, remember, greater efficiency means that the fuel used to develop a specific amount of power output is reduced, so that smaller fuel tanks, longer flights, and less cost are all benefits of greater efficiency.

15

Throttle response

One of the benefits least appreciated is that of improved throttle response and a generally more tolerant idle and mid-range throttle setting found with four-strokes. Some four-strokes are not, however, too easy to set up for top-end mixture setting, though more recent engines are better than the earlier models. In the absence of hard fact, I can only suppose that the improvement in carburettor performance is partially due to higher gas velocity through smaller diameter carburettor bores and partially due to the relatively short inlet tract length of the four-stroke when compared with the tortuous path the gases follow from carburettor to combustion chamber in the two-stroke.

Disadvantages

It is only fair to the long established two-stroke to point out that there are disadvantages to the four-stroke: be aware of them and your relationship with your motor will be all the more satisfying. First of these must be cost. Cost is related to complexity and, by established model engine standards, the four-stroke is a complex piece of machinery. There are many more working parts including in most instances gears and cams, both of which need to be made with precision if they are to do their job properly. Of course, more working parts means more working parts wearing out, increasing maintenance costs. The greater complexity also adds to the weight of the motor and in early four-strokes this greater weight and low power output really was a major disadvantage, but it is less so now with better power outputs.

The greater problems of corrosion that beset four-strokes (unlike the two-stroke which only suffers slightly from this phenomenon) could be thought to be a disadvantage, too. The crankcase of the two-

The original O.S. FS-60, forerunner of many other commercial four-strokes, shown sectioned at an exhibition.

A large-scale Sopwith *Pup* taxiing out for take-off. Interest in large models and the introduction of four-strokes made a happy coincidence.

stroke is continuously flushed out with fuel and oil mixture and unless very high nitro-methane fuel is used, corrosion is not usually a problem. However, in a four-stroke a combination of lower crankcase temperature and no positive flushing out of the crankcase leaves corrosive by-products of combustion to condense in the crankcase, where after a very short period of time corrosion can take place. This occurrence has to be rigorously prevented by flushing out and applying oil to protect the parts; this whole matter is treated more thoroughly in a future chapter.

While trying to be fair to the two-stroke it should also be recognised that the route chosen by engine manufacturers towards greater power, that of increasing RPM, is a trap that four-stroke engine manufacturers could all too easily fall into. There is no reason whatsoever to suppose that the four-stroke has to be less powerful, less noisy and more economical than the two-stroke – the turbo-charged 1.5 litre Formula 1 racing car engine is extremely noisy, uses a terrifying quantity of fuel, turns at very high RPM and is very powerful!

On the other hand, were we to be happy to accept from a two-stroke the current power output levels produced by four-stroke engines, then I believe that a two-stroke could be designed that produced very similar characteristics in terms of noise and power as the four-stroke and it would be lighter and cheaper. Either route has its attractions, but as the purpose of this book is to unravel some of the mysteries of the four-stroke, from here on comparison will cease and we will come to grips with the more intricate details of the modern four-stroke model engine.

2 Valves and lubrication

Valve types, Poppet and rotary. Tappet adjustment. Valve bounce. Gear and belt operation of rotary valves. Other valve types. Lubrication of engine, method of oil circulation. Crankcase oil breather.

Precise timing of the cycle of admission and exhaust of the gases in the four-stroke has already been briefly mentioned and its importance in the areas of economy, overall efficiency, noise level and performance stressed. Exactly how the control is effected needs further description as there are many and varied means of operation of a multitude of valve types. The most important of these in model four-stroke engines are poppet and rotary valves.

Poppet valves
It seems sensible to commence with a description of the most common method found on the model engine, the Poppet Valve operated by a Camshaft either directly or via operating Pushrods. The usual arrangement of the poppet valve is in an Overhead position. See Figure 3 for illustration of the various poppet valve and camshaft layouts. Choice of this arrangement in preference to the Side Valve has been made for several reasons, notably the physical bulk of the engine and optimising the shape of the combustion chamber. Although the first reason is not critical in simple single cylinder engines where the camshaft position and inlet and outlet arangements are simple, the latter certainly is.

The classic description of the poppet valve is as being 'mushroom' shaped, meaning that there is a stem flaring out to a circular head of suitable diameter to block the valve port. The seal of the valve is effected by an angular contact face running round the circumference of the head seating on a matching angled seat machined into the cylinder head of the engine. The contact angle is likely to vary from 30 to 45°. In the interests of weight control, model engines are constructed largely from aluminium alloys which are not

18

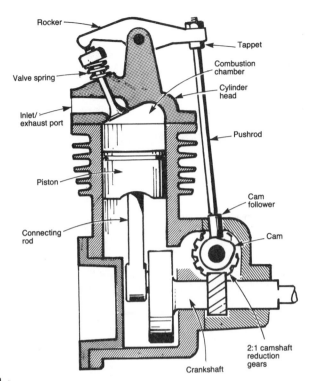

Fig. 3a

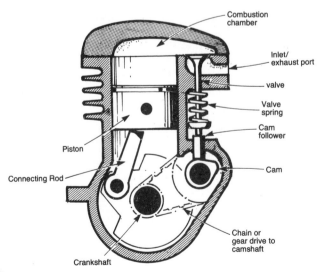

Fig. 3b

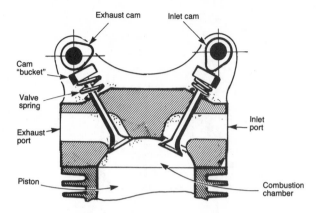

Exhaust cam   Inlet cam

Cam "bucket"

Valve spring

Inlet port

Exhaust port

Piston

Combustion chamber

Fig. 3c

suitable for the continual percussive action of the closing valve, so a seat of harder metal is usually inserted into the cylinder head, which may also be shaped to act as a bearing or guide for the valve. See Figure 4. A close seal is obtained by grinding the valve to match the seat in situ.

The valve is usually held closed by means of a spring, the so-called Valve Spring, which can be a coil, leaf or hairpin spring, though most commonly a coil is used.

The critical opening of the poppet valve is effected by a cam which also controls the timing of the valve. The four-stroke will have two valves per cylinder, each requiring a separate cam, and the two cams are mounted on a camshaft driven from the engine crankshaft in a precise relationship by gears, chain, or toothed timing belt. As each valve only opens and closes once during the two-revolution four-

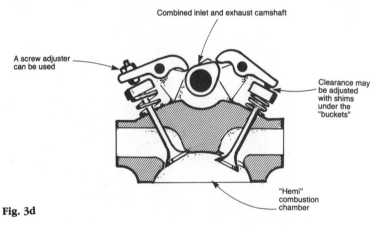

Combined inlet and exhaust camshaft

A screw adjuster can be used

Clearance may be adjusted with shims under the "buckets"

"Hemi" combustion chamber

Fig. 3d

20

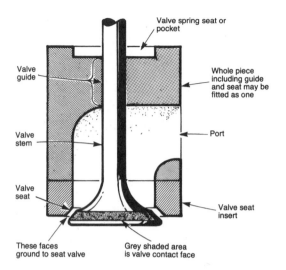

Valve spring seat or pocket

Valve guide

Whole piece including guide and seat may be fitted as one

Valve stem

Port

Valve seat

Valve seat insert

Fig. 4

These faces ground to seat valve

Grey shaded area is valve contact face

stroke cycle, the camshaft is driven at half the crankshaft speed. This can lead to some confusion when the camshafts are examined: because the timing cycles are expressed in terms of degrees of rotation of the crankshaft and as the camshaft rotates at half crankshaft speed, it is easy to see that it appears to open the valves for twice as long as it should do. A typical timing diagram for a model four-stroke is shown as Figure 5 and also a corresponding inlet cam.

Positioning of the camshaft is not merely a matter of fashion, for there are very sound reasons why the cam should be placed in one location or another. From the strict performance and efficiency point of view, the Overhead Camshaft (OHC) location is most

A cylinder head showing the combustion chamber and valves. Third dark area is of course the plug entry.

21

Fig. 5a

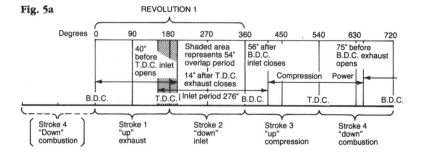

favoured. Firstly there is an absolutely direct operation of the valve with no intervening linkages between camshaft and valve to lose motion or precision of timing and there are no additional losses of power through Cam Followers, Pushrods or actuating Rockers. The classic arrangement for full-size engines is the Double or Twin Overhead Cam (DOHC or TOHC), one camshaft operating inlet and the other exhaust valves. A favoured compromise is the Single Overhead Cam. (SOHC) operating the valves through rockers or, if the valves are arranged in a side by side layout, they can be operated directly. See Figure 6.

The disadvantage of this system from the model point of view is really one of engine height and cylinder head complexity, plus the need for a longer drive train from crankshaft to camshaft, effectively adding extra parts to the engine and complicating its manufacture.

Fig. 5b

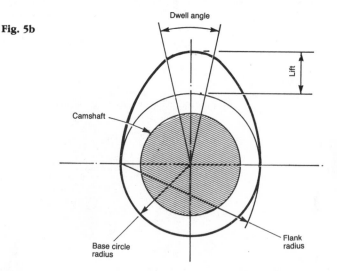

Fig.6

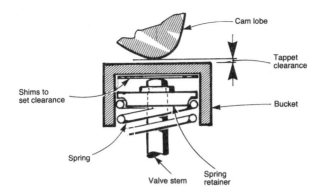

By far the most common system in use is the pushrod-operated Overhead Valve (OHV) with the camshaft gear driven directly from the crankshaft using a gear mounted on the main crankshaft (as seen in OS and Saito products) or via a reduction gear driven by the crankpin to the rear of the engine (as seen in Enya and Laser engines).

Because of the numerous points between cam and valve where parts have what is effectively a 'free' form of contact there is a build-up of clearances which, when considered alongside the varying materials used for manufacture of the parts, each with a different coefficient of linear expansion, can be seen to present quite a lot of scope for variance between *ideal* valve timing and actual valve timing and it is a demanding task for the designer of a miniature four-stroke to optimise the valve operation. With very small openings of the valves the dramatic effect on amount of movement that can be caused by excessive clearances obviously needs to be allowed for.

The component parts of a pushrod overhead valve system. Note the cams on the small gears, which are driven by the crankshaft extension, centre.

This is done by adjusters on the rockers, known as Tappets. Adjustment may be made either with the engine hot or cold, depending on the manufacturer's specification. Accuracy is essential – too small a clearance and the valve may not close properly, too large and the opening period of the valve will be shortened. This point will be covered more fully in a later chapter.

So much for the poppet valve. The above broad description of the type will vary in detail from particular engine to particular engine but the principle remains the most widely used and understood in use.

Demands for higher power in four-strokes plus the precision manufacturing needed by the camshaft-operated poppet valve have led model engine manufacturers to look at possible alternatives. There are definitely disadvantages to poppet valves, mostly concerned with the valve springs, which may not be capable of closing the valve sufficiently rapidly at very high RPM, leading to the condition known as 'valve float', and there may also be 'valve bounce' whereby the inertia of the valve causes it to rebound from the seat opening at a second and inappropriate time. Both phenomena limit the RPM of the engine and can be heard on existing model engines if the model in put into a high speed full throttle drive. Either occurrence can damage the engine as the valves may strike the piston if they are open at the wrong time. A possible solution in the form of a mechanical closure system known as a Desmodromic valve was developed for racing motor bikes and used by the Italian Ducati company to some effect, but this adds complexity as there are numerous parts required in the complete valve system from crankshaft gear through to the valve itself.

Camshaft arrangement with a toothed belt drive. Rocker arms and tappets can be seen in central groove across cylinder head.

The bottom end of the valve assembly shown 'exploded' on page 23. The crankshaft extension and cam gear shafts engage in the bearings in the crankcase cover.

Rotary valves

Rotary valves appear to be a very practical and simple alternative. After all, they are found in just about every two-stroke currently on the market, in crankshaft rotary, disc or drum valve versions. In principle the four-stroke rotary valve operates in just the same way as the familiar crankshaft rotary valve, except that the valve only rotates at half the crankshaft speed. This system has not found practical favour for full-size engines running on pure petrol fuels, but in model sizes the powerful cooling effect of the methanol fuel and its generous oil content serve together to lubricate and cool the rotary valve in a way that is entirely impractical with the full-size. (By the same token, the exotic materials needed to produce poppet valves that will withstand the temperatures of petrol fuels are not needed in model sizes, quite 'ordinary' steels will suffice.)

Two different arrangements of rotary valve porting are found in the model four-stroke world, the single ported valve as on the Austrian HP engines and the multiple ported valve as seen on Webra and the Condor engines. A further variation was used on the short-lived Newstock engine in the form of a disc valve.

HP first introduced the single port rotary valve on an engine of 0.21 cu.in. capacity, the lower specific output of the four-stroke making it seem a total non-starter in the performance stakes if conventional (by then) poppet valves and moderate operating RPM had been chosen. The valve rotates about the vertical axis of the cylinder and is driven by a combination of bevel gears at the crankshaft and spur gears at the valve proper. The inlet, exhaust and a port for the glow-plug are arranged at 90° intervals around the

25

Fig. 7

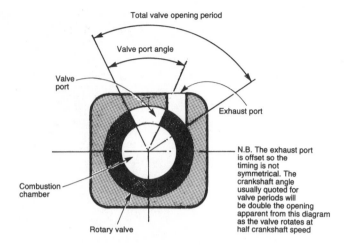

Total valve opening period

Valve port angle

Valve port

Exhaust port

N.B. The exhaust port is offset so the timing is not symmetrical. The crankshaft angle usually quoted for valve periods will be double the opening apparent from this diagram as the valve rotates at half crankshaft speed

Combustion chamber

Rotary valve

periphery of the cylinder, giving the valve a practical cycle of: admission, followed by a 90° rotation of the closed valve for compression, then the port opens to the glow-plug for ignition, leaving the power stroke and the exhaust stroke to follow during the remaining 180° of rotation of the valve. See Figure 7.

This is a very simple control method but one which demands clever design in angle, shape and opening diameters in all three cylinder ports and the valve port, with attention to the lubrication arrangements for both valve and its drive train gears.

The Cross type overhead rotary valve, running on an axis parallel to that of the crankshaft, has been chosen by Webra for their most recent four-stroke engines following a less than successful attempt to use an Aspin type rotary valve on their first commercial four-stroke. Although operating in a broadly similar manner to that of the HP, the Webra valve admits fuel/air through one port and allows exhaust through a separate port, thus making individual control of the timing of both phases of operation a simpler design task and, furthermore, making for far simpler drive. Both Webra and Condor use the simple expedient of a toothed timing belt running up the front of the engine driven by a crankshaft pulley. This type of valve may be arranged to admit and exhaust either through the ends or through sideways facing ports, the choice being really dependent on the practicality of siting the carburettor and exhaust pipes.

Other valve types

The valve types described cover those engines now in manufacturing production and widely available to the modeller, but there are other types that have seen the light of day in model form.

26

Bevel-driven rotary valve as used on HP and Webra engines. This arrangement makes for a compact unit with no external components.

Several modellers have made single examples of Sleeve Valve engines, a valve system that found considerable favour with full-size aircraft engine manufacturers because of its reliability when contrasted with the poppet valve with all its inherent weaknesses. The sleeve valve is, as its name implies, a tubular sleeve which wraps around the top part of the engine cylinder with valve ports that coincide with ports in the cylinder proper as the sleeve is either

A three-cylinder sleeve-valve engine of very neat appearance constructed by J. J. Griffiths and G. Cromm.

rotated or raised up and down by a cam. Although fit, finish, lubrication and heat dissipation present problems for this type of valve, the only moving parts are the sleeve and cam, plus a single reduction gear from crankshaft to cam, of course. In purely mechanical terms an engine fitted with this type of valve is only slightly more complex than the two-stroke and has much to commend it. It must only be a matter of time before such an engine finds its way into serious model-form production.

Slide, piston and reed valves, used in other small engine designs, do not appear to offer anything for four-strokes.

Lubrication

All through the above there have been mentions of the problems of lubrication. Wherever two parts of an engine are required to run together there will be a need for a film of lubricant to separate them. The lubricant, usually some form of oil, has the dual role of preventing contact and carrying away heat from moving parts. Although the model four-stroke operates at generally lower RPM than its two-stroke counterpart, there are still stringent demands made on a lubrication system.

Turning to full-size engines for a moment, the lubricating oil is usually contained in the crankcase of the engine or in a separate oil tank from which it is pumped to the engine, frequently via an oil cooler. Once inside the engine the oil is pumped under pressure to the places where it is required. Model engines operate on a much more haphazard arrangement (with the exception of the Kavan FK-50) in that the oil is mixed with the fuel and drawn into the engine through the carburettor, thus ensuring that the valves and piston/cylinder obtain a reasonable supply of oil.

The Kavan FK-50 takes advantage of the best from both worlds by using an oil filled sump with pump, dip-stick and oil scraper rings fitted to the pistons, but also recommending a 2% castor oil content to the fuel.

But what of the remaining parts of the engine? Even with the possibility of incredibly precise manufacturing tolerances available to him, the manufacturer must allow a working clearance between piston and cylinder and it is through this very small gap that oil is driven down to the lower crankcase to lubricate cams, gears, crankshaft and crankshaft bearings. Evidence of the passage of oil through these tiny spaces is always available from the crankcase breather of the engine, from which a tiny trickle of oil will usually be found emerging. The crankcase breather forms an essential role here, allowing excess oil to vent from the crankcase but more

A neatly-hidden engine in a scale model. Only the rockers and the 'extra' exhaust pipe are really noticeable. Scale cooling is a possibility with such a layout.

importantly preventing any build up of pressure in the crankcase that could deter the necessary oil from finding its way past the piston.

There is only one other known exception to the oil in the fuel principle of modern model four-stroke operation and that is the Swedish made Damo engine, for which a no-oil fuel is recommended. The manufacturer has minimised the need for additional oil by such means as fitting roller bearings to the big and little ends of the connecting rod and specially selecting the alloys used for the piston and cylinder. It is felt that the very slight lubricating properties of the methanol fuel itself are adequate for normal operation and independent tests seem to bear out the manufacturer's claims. Even with such an engine it is unlikely that any performance drop would be experienced and I for one would feel perfectly justified in ignoring the 'no oil' instructions and adding 2-3% oil to the fuel.

3 Practical considerations

Choice of engine-size, power, weight. Fuel consumption and tank size. Propeller sizes. Ancillary equipment, propeller material, balancing and fitting. Test stands and engine mounting. Starting technique, adjustment and running-in. In-air running-in.

In spite of the variety and layout of the numerous motors operating on the four-stroke principle, choice of a particular motor for any model application need not be governed by these factors. Although there has been only a comparatively short period of development of these motors, commercial pressures have resulted in a situation where the major manufacturers all market immensely practical and reliable products. If a sports model is your choice then select a motor with a capacity that best suits your model. If scale modelling is your idea of heaven, then you may have some constraints on your choice of motor.

Such factors as height, length, weight or just plain shape may influence your choice of motor, particularly where there is a cowled-in installation. A visit to the local stockist of the motor of your choice with either your model plan or a tracing of the nose area, even the cowling if you already have it to hand, will answer the question of 'will it fit?'

If there is a choice of engine size, always go for the most powerful. A lack of power is a distinct embarrassment, too much and you can always throttle back! For many scale models weight of the engine can be a problem. Many existing designs are intended for two-stroke engines and the constructional methods chosen reflect the weight of this type of engine being fixed to the front of the model. This is unlikely to be a problem with many early biplane designs, most of which would probably finish up tail-heavy with many two-stroke engines; the additional weight of the four-stroke will help to bring the balance point to a suitable position. Nor need you worry in this situation about the overall weight of the model, since it would almost certainly have been necessary to add weight to the nose of the model to bring the balance point forward if a two-stroke were to have been fitted.

Of course the opposite case applies if the model has a long nose to start with! If the model is non-scale it is sometimes possible to shorten the nose a little to help, but this is not really an acceptable possibility with a scale model. Here it may well be that weight dictates choice of engine. Do remember that the weight of some two-strokes may not be quoted with silencer and the four-stroke silencer if fitted is quite rudimentary and weighs only a fraction of that fitted to a two-stroke.

By choosing a larger capacity motor you will also go some way towards making up for the lower specific power output of the four-stroke, although in most biplane models, and many monoplanes come to that, the model would probably have been grossly overpowered with a two-stroke at the top of the design capacity range.

An often unremarked benefit of the four-stroke is that as a result of its lower fuel consumption, the fuel tank fitted may be of a smaller size, probably about half the size normally fitted to the model. This also means that there will be more flexibility in the detailed design of the front end of the model and models that could only house marginally sized fuel tanks for two-strokes, or that needed a

Short noses are normal with WW1 fighters and even the radio batteries are as far forward as possible on this model. Dummy cylinders simulate rotary engine of prototype.

compromise on fuel tank position, can now be tackled in a more satisfactory manner. There are some minor attendant problems in this area, however, as the carburettor on the four-stroke will often be fitted to the engine in a position that makes optimum fuel tank alignment difficult. More on this aspect of operations in a later chapter.

Propeller size for any given capacity four-stroke will be at least 1 inch (25 mm) larger, which may not seem like a big problem, but the extra 12 mm can make all the difference on ground clearance for take-off on rough ground.

In order, then, the considerations that need to be made when choosing your new engine are:

(a) Power. This usually means capacity. At least 25% extra capacity for a four-stroke if the engine size quoted for any chosen model is for a two-stroke. In smaller size models, though, modern 0.60 cu.in. four-strokes are virtually as powerful as the two-strokes of ten years ago.

(b) Weight, where cowling is not a consideration.

(c) Physical size. Will it fit into the model?

(d) Position of carburettor, which may be a minor problem.

If all other things are equal, at this point there may be a choice between engines with differing construction or valve types and then

Multi-cylinder four-strokes make capturing the atmosphere of 1920/30s exposed radial engines automatic, as on this Saro 'Cloud' amphibian. If, of course, you can afford them!

Another exposed-engine prototype, the Handley-Page HP42 1930s airliner. Four engines on this one, but two could be dummies. Sounds superb in the air.

maybe maintenance should be next on the list, followed by price and aesthetic considerations, with constructional details last of all.

Making your purchase

When you actually purchase your engine it is a very good idea to purchase propellers of suitable size and material, a glow-plug if necessary and suitable fuel. All my previous experience with model engines had until recently led me to shun the use of electric starters, but I have to confess to finding that four-strokes do not lend themselves to my well-developed two-stroke flicking technique and I have now come down firmly in favour of using an electric starter. Do not be put off this course of action by die-hard modellers who have been handling engines for many years. They have probably forgotten how difficult they found starting engines when they began modelling. I see no virtue in making a tricky task more difficult than it need be when there is equipment readily available to simplify matters.

Nor should you be alarmed by wild stories of badly damaged engines resulting from the use of electric starters. A fool will damage his engine electric starter or not, and by following a few sensible precautions you will not damage your engine and enjoy flying and not frustration. If you do buy a starter, until you are used to its operation I recommend the use of a small spinner on the engine, which will make solid engagement of the rubber cup of the starter easier to achieve. A source of power for the glow-plug will also be needed and a connector to couple plug to glow battery. A 2 volt rechargeable battery of 2-3 Ampere Hour capacity will be needed and with many four-strokes, the normal type of 'snap-on' glow connector will not fit, or at least will fit but because the glow-plug is fitted to the front of the cylinder leaning forward, will foul the propeller. You may be able to find a connector that is sufficiently compact to clear the propeller arc when in use, but the solution is likely to be 'crocodile' clips initially and a permanently wired up glow-plug when the engine is finally installed in a model.

Propellers

To return to propellers, these should be wooden or 'glass-filled' plastic for any four-stroke over 0.40 cu.in. capacity for reasons of safety, and even with engines below 0.40 cu.in. there are sound reasons for choosing these types of propeller, primarily because the noise levels generated by rigid propellers have been found to be lower than those generated by more flexible plastic types.

Because of the more widely spaced, more violent power strokes of the four-stroke, the propeller blades are constantly subjected to fierce acceleration and then the strong braking effect of air resistance. This repeated reversal of stresses in the propeller blade roots will cause fatigue failure in a relatively short period of time if plain, unreinforced plastic propellers are used.

There is something to be said for recommending exclusive use of reinforced plastic propellers, for in addition to the blade fatigue

Fig. 8

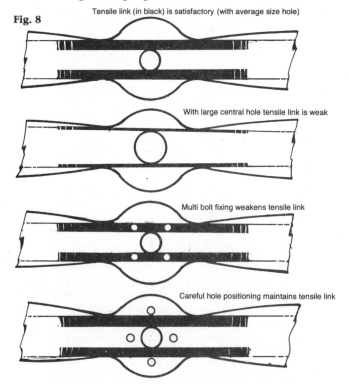

Tensile link (in black) is satisfactory (with average size hole)

With large central hole tensile link is weak

Multi bolt fixing weakens tensile link

Careful hole positioning maintains tensile link

An assortment of propellers from 12 to 18 inches diameter in wood and glass-filled plastic, the safest and quietest materials for propellers.

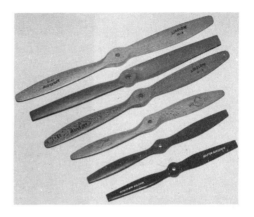

problem, there is an attendant problem of hub crushing associated with wooden propellers. The sharp load reversals that lead to failure of plastic propellers tempt the engine user to progressively tighten the propeller retaining nut and the compressible wood steadily crushes under the pressure. Nor is the fitting of driver pins or multiple bolt fixing a ready solution here. Wood has a grain structure that has to go from tip to tip of the propeller if it is to have any strength at all, and drive pins will inevitably tend to create a splitting force on the wood of the propeller. At the very least, great care should be taken to position the propeller so that the drive pins are best located. If there is a choice between propellers of the same type and different manufacture, always choose the example with the most substantial hub. See Figure 8.

As far as size is concerned, choose the smallest recommended propeller for the engine. This may seem at first to be rather strange advice, but the prime requirements for running in are that the engine should turn over fast, remain cool and well lubricated but not

Propeller balance can be achieved by sanding one blade or varnishing the other, checking on a balance device such as this, or with a dowel or bolt supported by knife-edges.

Fig. 9

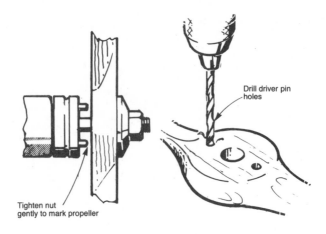

Drill driver pin holes

Tighten nut gently to mark propeller

be overloaded. By fitting a small propeller the engine can be run with a rich fuel mixture at normal operating RPM. This lightly loaded rich running allows the engine to settle down well but remain cool and well lubricated.

With any model engine a properly balanced propeller is recommended. Even mass produced plastic propellers will almost certainly be out of balance as supplied. Firstly drill or ream the centre hole so that it fits the crankshaft properly. The best system to use is to drill the propeller in a pillar drill so that the hole through the centre remains square to the blades. Do not drill the hole over-size, as this will make the propeller difficult to mount and even if the blades are balanced carefully it will certainly run out of balance. Either purchase a proper balancing device or find an appropriate sized spindle to fit the hole in the hub and set the propeller up on two parallels. Balance by thinning the heavier blade; do not trim the

Two engines fitted with drive pins. Note left-hand one uses a tubular prop-retaining nut, that on the right a split tapered collet nut.

Fig. 10

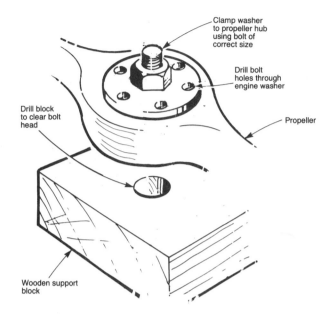

Clamp washer to propeller hub using bolt of correct size

Drill bolt holes through engine washer

Propeller

Drill block to clear bolt head

Wooden support block

ends off the heavy blade. If the propeller is a varnished type it may be preferable to achieve a satisfactory balance by applying additional coats of fuel-proof varnish to the lighter blade until it balances.

For engines fitted with drive pins first ream the hole to suit the crankshaft then slip the propeller into place, applying light pressure to the hub by lightly tightening the propeller retaining nut until the drive pins mark the drive face of the hub. Remove the propeller and you will find that the positions of the drive holes have been impressed on the drive face, providing an exact guide for drilling the holes. See Figure 9.

For multiple bolt fixings, use a bolt of the same size as the crankshaft to locate the drilled clamping washer against the front face of the propeller and then use the holes in the washer as a drilling jig to drill the holes. See Figure 10.

Running
Many fuel manufacturers now make fuel formulated specifically for four-stroke engines, but even so the individual engine manufacturer's instructions should be followed with regard to fuel type. A regular feature of four-stroke fuel is its lower than normal (in modelling terms) oil content. Beware of using fuel with too high an oil content, which can have bad effects on the running characteristics of a four-stroke motor. You will find more in-depth information on fuel formulas in a later chapter, but for the moment

37

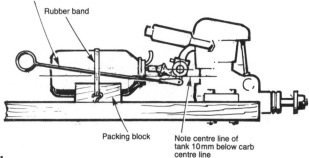

Trap throttle wire under rubber band

Rubber band

Packing block

Note centre line of tank 10mm below carb centre line

Fig. 11

during running in use a good quality commercially blended fuel with only a low nitro-methane content. Providing care is taken, there is no reason why either synthetic or vegetable oil (castor oil) should not be used.

Once the necessary propeller has been selected, balanced and fitted, plus of course the recommended spinner, the engine should be fitted to a suitable test stand for first runs. There are sound reasons for using a test stand if this is a first engine, but if it is not then there are equally good reasons for fitting it straight into your model. Assuming that it is a first engine, a period of operation on a solid test stand with all the necessary accessories close to hand will help to familiarise you with the engine before it is fitted into the more awkward environment of the actual model.

Either one of the several ready-made test stands or a purpose-made wooden version tailored to suit the particular engine can be used. Whichever route you choose to follow, make sure that it is substantial enough for the engine. A 0.40 cu.in. engine should be mounted on at least ⅜ inch square (10 mm) hardwood bearers with absolutely minimum overhang. Larger engines need ½ inch square for 0.60 cu.in. and by the time that capacity reaches the 0.90 cu.in level and over, metal test stands start to become a necessity unless very large wooden beams are to be used.

Fixing bolts should be the largest size that will go through the holes in the engine mounting lugs, typically 6 BA for 0.40 cu.in., 4 BA for 0.60 cu.in., etc, as the capacity rises. Material for bolts would be standard mild steel: use of high tensile bolts is not really necessary and in the event of a crash, these very strong bolts may not shear, as the weaker mild steel bolts can, and crankcase damage may result.

Do fix the fuel tank to the test stand securely, as a loose fuel tank will be blown about by the propeller slipstream and in the excitement of the first start-up reaching for a wayward fuel tank may

38

A sturdy metal test stand with well-secured fuel tank and adequate clearances for good accessibility, welded to a heavy base plate.

result in an accident. The same goes for the throttle lever, arrange for a suitable extension to this so that the throttle may be operated safely from the rear of the engine, and preferably arrange some form of friction fitting so that the throttle remains where it is put during extended running-in periods. It may be necessary to prop up the tank so that it is at the correct level, which should be with the tank centre-line around ³⁄₈ inch below that of the carburettor centre line. See Figure 11.

Now that the engine is mounted and the necessary tank, throttle, glow-plug connector and starter are to hand, fill up the tank and prepare to start up. Most four-stroke motors start best with the throttle closed or almost closed. The suction available is limited and a wide-open throttle makes it difficult for some engines to draw fuel. The sequence of events is as follows:

(a) Open the main fuel mixture control needle valve in accordance with the manufacturer's instructions. If there are no instructions, then open the needle valve 3 turns from fully closed. It is as well to check that the 'closed' position corresponds with the 'screwed right down' position. It is not unknown for the needle valve to need to be unscrewed 2 or 3 turns from the shut right down position before it actually admits any fuel. If this is the case then open the needle valve three turns from the point where it actually admits fuel. This latter point can easily be checked by attaching a piece of fuel tubing to the fuel inlet nipple and blowing down it to ascertain when the needle valve actually opens.

(b) If there is a choke fitted, close this and rotate the propeller anti-clockwise when viewed from the front and watch the fuel line. You should see the fuel rise up the line to the carburettor. Once the fuel has reached the carburettor,

39

continue to crank for a few more turns to draw some fuel into the combustion chamber. Many four-strokes like to be quite wet to start up, but beware of excessive choking, which can fill the combustion chamber with raw fuel and cause a hydraulic lock as the engine is turned over, possibly damaging the engine. If there is any sign that this has occurred, loosen the glow-plug and turn the engine over a few times to drive out the excess fuel.

(c) With the throttle closed connect up the glow-plug and grasp the propeller firmly and turn over the engine. You should feel a distinct kick as the piston goes over top dead centre indicating that there is fuel present and that there is a glow at the plug firing the mixture. At this point hand starting techniques and electric starter techniques need explaining. If you are using an electric starter then the previous step is absolutely essential as the power available from the starter will easily overcome a considerable resistance and damage the engine if it is flooded with fuel. On no account should the starter be applied while the choke flap is closed, since this will result in a flooded engine with serious risk of damage. If all is well, a brief application of the starter will start up the engine. Hand starting is a matter of trial and error, you can either flick the engine over compression in its normal running direction (anti-clockwise) or turn the engine backwards towards compression then smartly bounce flick the engine back against compression upon which it will fire and run in a correct clockwise direction. In either case, a rubber finger protector is advised.

(d) If you are fortunate, the engine will fire and continue to run slowly, and you can attempt to speed up by opening the throttle slightly. Assuming that it continues to run then progressively open the throttle, noting the sound and appearance of the exhaust which should be smoky and 'throaty' indicating that the mixture is good and rich. The engine may cut out as soon as you open the throttle in one of two ways. A brief burst of power followed by the engine dying cleanly away with no excess of smoke or unburnt fuel from the exhaust indicates a weak mixture. Open the main mixture control needle valve a little and try again. If the engine dies with an excess of fuel and a lot of smoke, weaken the fuel mixture a little by closing the needle valve slightly.

(e) Once it is running fast and rich try removing the glow-plug battery connection. If it stops, then it is probably still too rich. Close the throttle, re-connect the glow-plug and re-start adjusting the needle valve for a weaker mixture.

(f) With a smooth rich full throttle run established allow the motor to run for about five minutes then stop it, allow it to cool and repeat the runs until 15-20 minutes running have accumulated.

(g) Fit the flying size propeller and start up again. You will almost certainly have to re-adjust the needle valve but leave the mixture rich still. Try leaning the mixture out after a couple of 5-minute runs on the larger propeller, but if there is any sign of labouring or overheating, close the throttle and open the needle valve again. Continue the short rich mixture runs until the engine will consistently run with the throttle wide open and the mixture still on the rich side. Fully lean full throttle running should not be attempted until the engine has an hour or so of running time accumulated.

By this time the engine should have settled down enough to throttle quite well. Check the setting of the idle mixture by opening the throttle rapidly from the idle setting. It should pick up smoothly and cleanly. If it does not and dies as the throttle is opened quickly, then the idle mixture is too weak. If the engine is fitted with an air-bleed type carburettor, indicated by a small hole on the front of the carburettor and an adjusting screw which blocks off the hole, then

Using an electric starter, which has to be pressed firmly against the propeller boss or spinner and thus needs the model to be held firmly.

41

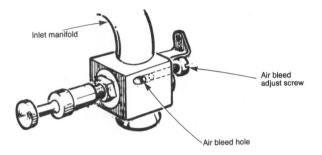

Inlet manifold

Air bleed
adjust screw

Air bleed hole

Fig. 12

turn the screw in so that it blocks off more of the air bleed, thus richening the mixture. See Figure 12. Those carburettors with an idle mixture control needle valve, characterised by having a second adjusting needle opposite the fuel inlet jet, need to have the second needle opened to allow more fuel into the carburettor. See Figure 13. The principle of altering the mixture strength is opposite in the two different types of carburettor: in the former type the air flow is altered, in the second type the fuel flow is controlled.

The alternative to the abrupt weak mixture stop is the slow, smoky, uneven acceleration indicating a rich idle mixture. Correct this by either opening the air bleed screw or closing down the idle mixture control.

There is nothing wrong with circumventing the tedious bench running process and installing the new engine straight into a model

Two types of air bleed carburettor, identical in operation though differing in physical layout. Air bleed hole is clearly visible on both.

42

Fig. 13

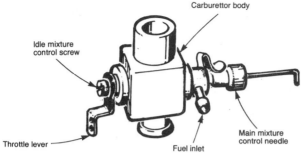

and running it in while flying, provided that the model is well flown and the operator totally conversant with its flying characteristics. An unflown scale model and a new four-stroke are however a combination that will potentially provide problems for the most experienced. At the very least, sufficient fuel should be run through the engine to free it off enough to provide a reasonable idle and reliable if rich full power. In-the-air running in should be thoroughly and sensibly carried out. Set the motor rich, on no account strive for maximum power and preferably fit a slightly finer pitch than normal propeller.

Once you are satisfied that the engine will keep going and provide adequate power for safe flight, allow the engine to cool, re-fuel, start up and get airborne as quickly as practical. Throttle back as soon as a safe altitude is reached and continue to fly using the throttle freely, never letting the engine labour and avoiding aerobatics and steep climbs until the first hour's running has been completed. In an ideal world in-air running in would be a solo operation, as the sound of the engine is a sure indicator of potential trouble and whilst other models are flying, the naturally quiet note of the four-stroke can easily be blanketed out.

Whichever method of running in you choose to follow, there is little doubt that a careful and thorough job will be of long-term benefit to the engine, which will reward you by giving long and reliable service.

43

4 Mountings and fuel supply

Types of engine mount, plastic or metal? Cutting threads in metal mounts. Front bulkhead rigidity and weight. Bolt materials. Fuel tank positions, fuel pumps. Tank pressurisation. Glow-plug heating circuits for multi-cylinder engines. Fuel filtering.

There is no doubt that the four-stroke engine demands more care and thought in installation than simpler two-stroke motors. This is particularly true of the larger capacity motors that present almost as many demands on their operators as a full-size aircraft engine.

First runs of the engine described in Chapter 3 will have a permanent effect on the engine and unless they are carried out with care, the most thorough attention to detail in the future will not repair early damage. Mention has been made of the need for a solid mounting for the engine and there are various ways of achieving this.

Types of engine mount
The majority of four-stroke engines up to and including single cylinder engines of around 1.2 cu.in. capacity are designed to be fitted to beam mounts,. Some larger engines, particularly those with two and more cylinders, are fitted with integral radial mounts so that the engine may be fitted directly to a flat bulkhead without the need to fit first to a mount of some type.

There is no doubt in my mind that cast or machined aluminium alloy mounts are the most satisfactory means of fixing an engine into a model aircraft. If a plastic mount has to be used for some reason, then it must be moulded from a glass reinforced plastic. As already explained when referring to propellers, there are powerful acceleration and deceleration forces involved in the four-stroke cycle which as well as being transmitted to the propeller are also transmitted to the engine mount and airframe. Non-reinforced plastic mounts have been known to fail under the stresses of quite small capacity four-stroke motors.

44

An example of a glass reinforced plastic mounting. These can be satisfactory if moulded with adequate reinforcement but plain plastic mouldings are best avoided.

Although the crankcase of a model engine appears to be relatively solid in build, it is not difficult to distort by fixing the engine to a mount which is not true. Always inspect a metal mount to see that the mounting surfaces have been machine-finished after casting and are not left 'as cast'. There are some mounts available, notably OS Products own brand, that are pressure die-cast and are thus as accurately finished as those that are machined following casting. There is a particular advantage to be had in using OS mounts in that they are ready drilled and tapped (holes threaded) for fitting to OS engines and may well fit other manufacturers' products as well. They are however expensive in comparison with a more 'do-it-yourself' approach.

It is certainly good practice to drill and tap in the metal mount rather than drill holes right through the mount and then use nuts

Using an engineer's square to check that the tap remains vertical when threading a metal mount. Can also be used to align a drill.

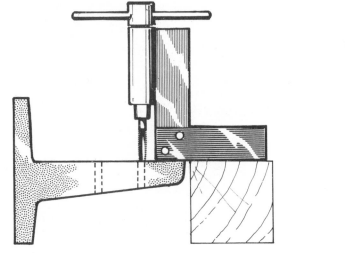

Fig. 14

and washers to secure the engine. The procedure is not difficult but does require the purchase of some items of special equipment. You will need:

(a) Drill of suitable size for a thread to be cut on the inside (tapping size drill) – see table.
(b) A tap wrench for holding and turning the tap.
(c) A tap of appropriate size, see table for guide to fixing bolt sizes.
(d) Lubricant for thread cutting – paraffin is good for aluminium alloys.

Table 1

Thread size	Clearance size drill	Tapping size drill
6 BA	2.9 mm	2.3 mm
4 BA	3.7 mm	3.0 mm
3 mm	3.1 mm	2.5 mm
4 mm	4.1 mm	3.3 mm
5 mm	5.1 mm	4.2 mm

A proper drill press is an advantage but care and use of a square against the drill to guide the accurate drilling of the holes can substitute, as shown in the photograph. Mark out the positions of the mounting holes directly onto the mount, using a scriber or some other sharp instrument that will mark the metal, or first put a strip of masking tape on the mount then use a pencil. Select the correct size drill for the thread size chosen and drill the four holes. You will be best advised to obtain a 'second cut' tap, which will be recognisable by the tapered end and will cut a full thread in through holes, but not in 'blind' holes. See Figure 14. Grip the tap in the tap wrench and apply some paraffin to both tap and mount, then insert the tap into the hole and, applying a little pressure, start to screw the tap into the hole in the mount.

As the tap starts to bite and cut the thread use great caution. It is very easy to try to achieve too many turns of thread too quickly and end up breaking the tap. Every turn forward should be followed by a quarter turn back so that the chips of metal are broken up and don't clog up and jam the tap. After five or six turns take the tap right out of the hole, clean, and reapply lubricant before reinserting and continuing the thread cutting.

As soon as the tap has cut a thread right through the mount, clean out the swarf from the hole, wipe all traces of swarf from the mount and then you are ready to fix the engine. It is important to clean up before fitting the engine as traces of metal swarf can very easily find their way into the engine, causing permanent damage. This is particularly important if the drilling and tapping of the mount is being carried out after the mount has been fitted into the model.

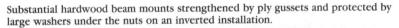

Substantial hardwood beam mounts strengthened by ply gussets and protected by large washers under the nuts on an inverted installation.

A method of mounting on wood bearers but using metal plates. Note the secondary plates beneath the bearers. Makes motor changes simple!

Drilling swarf can easily collect in little corners of the engine compartment and only start to blow around the first time the engine is started up, whereupon it will be sucked straight into the engine.

Of course, there is little point in making a first class job of fitting the engine to the mount if the mount is not in turn fitted to a flat bulkhead made of adequate thickness material, a minimum of 4 mm plywood for 0.40 cu.in. motors rising to 6 or 8 mm plywood for larger engines. One of the drawbacks of using this type of mounting system

Fig. 15

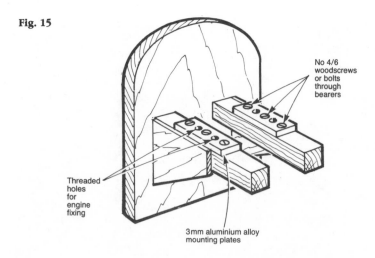

No 4/6 woodscrews or bolts through bearers

Threaded holes for engine fixing

3 mm aluminium alloy mounting plates

48

This radial mounting plate is stood off the engine by three spacers and also has large diameter spacers between it and the ply bulkhead, giving rather an overhang.

is that the most straightforward solution is to use a ply engine mount bulkhead, and on a model with a large frontal area the size of the piece of heavy plywood required gives a weight penalty out of all proportion to the strength requirements. Either more complex detail structural design around the nose of the model has to be considered or an alternative to the large ply plate bulkhead and metal mount has to be used.

My own preferred alternative in virtually every case is to use hardwood engine bearers glued securely into ply bulkheads supported with ply gussets wherever there is a substantial overhang. As well as producing a lighter nose structure, this method will result in a stiffer fuselage front end as the hardwood engine bearers extend back through two or three formers.

It is a good idea to fit threaded metal plates to the hardwood bearers so that the fixing bolts will not crush them. These can be of 3 mm (0.125 in.) aluminium alloy fixed to the bearers with small woodscrews. See Figure 15.

In either case, it is preferable to use mild steel or even brass bolts to fix the engine to the mount. In the unfortunate event of a crash, the softer bolts will shear whereas high tensile steel bolts, such as hexagon socket cap (Allen) bolts, will not and the mounting lugs on the engine may be damaged.

Fuel tank position
One major problem encountered by users of four-stroke motors relates to the positioning of the carburettor, which is almost always placed quite close to the cylinder head to keep the length of the inlet manifold to a minimum. This places the carburettor much further up from the centre line of the engine than desirable for installation

Fig. 16

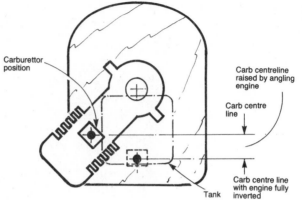

Carburettor position

Carb centreline raised by angling engine

Carb centre line

Carb centre line with engine fully inverted

Tank

purposes, with the result that it frequently becomes very difficult to fit the fuel tank in the ideal position relative to the carburettor. The centre line of the tank should be approximately 10 mm below that of the carburettor and if this relationship cannot be achieved there will always be compromises on fuel mixture setting required.

The frequently chosen means of achieving the line-up of carburettor and tank is to mount the engine at a 45° angle. See Figure 16. A less popular method would be to accept the unsatisfactory tank position and compensate by using a fuel pump. One manufacturer went as far as to fit a pump to his engine in acknowledgement of the problem. The Condor featured a peristaltic pump fixed to the end of the rotary valve spindle. A pump is, however, available that has proved reliable in use, the Micro Oscillator from Perry of the USA.

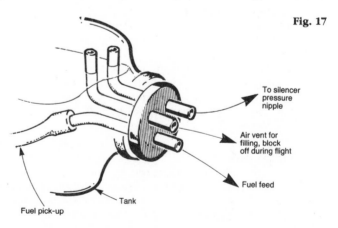

Fig. 17

To silencer pressure nipple

Air vent for filling, block off during flight

Fuel feed

Tank

Fuel pick-up

Fuel pump mounted on a bracket fitted to the crankcase and driven by a round belt from the head rotary valve, in turn driven by a toothed belt.

This very simple device uses the vibration of the engine to oscillate a piston back and forth in a tiny pump. It is important that the pump is placed correctly relative to the plane of vibration, that is to say with the axis of the pump across the fuselage. Properly sited, the Micro Oscillator will deliver the full fuel requirement for the largest four-stroke.

Pressurisation
Some degree of cure for badly positioned tanks can result from pressurising the tank from the exhaust of the engine. Most four-strokes are either supplied with a small exhaust silencer or such a silencer can be obtained as an extra. These silencers are usually fitted with a nipple intended to be used to connect to the fuel tank so that the pressure in the exhaust system can be used to pressurise the fuel tank. On no account should the crankcase breather nipple be used to pressurise the fuel tank: this must be kept completely clear at all times. See Figure 17 for the layout of an exhaust pressurised fuel system.

As soon as the fuel system is pressurised the effect will be immediately noticed on the carburettor settings. The pressure will increase the fuel flow through the carburettor both at full throttle and at idle and it will be necessary to adjust both controls.

51

When the HP 21 VT first appeared, the rotary valve lubrication was accomplished by coupling up the pressure nipple on the silencer supplied to a nipple on the cylinder head, fuel tank pressurisation being then effected by means of the breather nipple. In this instance the previous warning concerning the inadvisability of blocking the crankcase breather could be safely ignored, for the whole engine, crankcase included, was continuously purged by the throughflow of oily gases under pressure from the silencer. It was soon apparent to early operators of these engines that the needle valve was over-sensitive when silencer pressure was used but, conversely, there was inadequate fuel draw without the silencer pressure. The solution was to fit a T-piece in the pressure line from silencer to cylinder head, then couple up the fuel tank to this, leaving the crankcase nipple free to exhaust to atmosphere. This open circuit arrangement with the pressure split between fuel tank and lubrication duties totally cured fuel problems on the little HP.

The problems of too much pressure are not uncommon. Early four-stroke motors were regularly supplied with fuel mixture control needle valves with too fierce a taper, making motors that were quite practical to operate on the test bench super-critical in model aircraft flying. Addition of fuel pressurisation only aggravated the problem still further. Owners of early four-strokes that do seem very critical to adjust could look at more recent carburettor designs with possible benefit. It may only be necessary to replace the needle valve and jet supplied with a unit featuring either a shallower taper or a finer thread.

Glow-plug hook-ups

Particularly in the case of scale models featuring fully cowled-in engines, a means of connecting up the glow-plug without dismantling half the model will be needed. It is not altogether a bad idea with some non-scale models, either, to arrange a proper

The HP21 T-piece which cured early fuel problems. The small size of the silencer is apparent.

Fig. 18

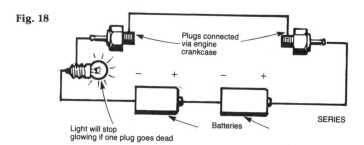

Plugs connected via engine crankcase

Light will stop glowing if one plug goes dead

Batteries

SERIES

Fig. 19

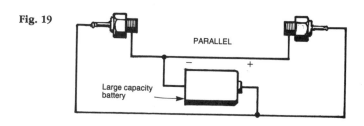

PARALLEL

Large capacity battery

connection system for the glow-plug for, on some engines, the position of the glow-plug does make using the conventional glow connector or clip hazardous.

There is something to be said for arranging for a glow-plug energising battery and switch system to be carried on board the model, actuated by the throttle servo when the throttle is closed. The glow ignition system does fail the engine at a far higher tick-over RPM than can be achieved if the plug is kept hot electrically. This is important with many lightly loaded models where the large propellers fitted to a typical four-stroke power plant will keep the model flying at the slowest tick-over speed attainable. This does make landing more difficult than it need be! It should be possible to slow the engine down by a further 500 RPM if the plug is kept hot.

In multi-cylinder installations a permanent circuit connecting up all the plugs to a single connection for the booster battery is essential. While it is possible to wire up all the glow-plugs in series and apply 1.5 volts per plug to the input end of the circuit, I would recommend that this method is not used, for if a short circuit occurs then all the plugs are likely to be blown instantly, an expensive business with a 5-cylinder radial. Instead, by connecting all the plugs in parallel and using a large capacity battery there will be no problems of this nature. If connected in series, a simple LED or meter can show instantly whether a plug has blown: dead plug equals no current flow at all and connecting plugs in parallel will still give an indication by lower current flow. Multi-cylinder engines may start and run quite well with a dead plug but it will nonetheless be very apparent from the reduced power and the unusual exhaust note. See Figures 18 and 19.

How ever the plugs are connected up to the energising source it is essential to have a reliable method of determining whether or not the plugs are actually glowing. An ammeter is the simplest way of doing this. It need not be at all accurate, the actual finite current flow is not important, what is important is that there is a current flowing! Variations in the current drawn by the plug can indicate the state of the engine, however. If the engine is flooded, the excess fuel in the cylinder will keep the glow-plug element cool and it will draw a higher than normal current. Conversely, a 'dry' engine will be indicated by a low current draw. Take mental note of the glow-plug current reading at which your engine reliably starts and use the information given by the ammeter to help diagnose problems.

Permanent wiring for the glow-plug in this model is attached to two bolts in the cowling which make convenient points on which to engage crocodile clips on the battery leads.

Clean fuel

Clean fuel is essential for reliable running of the engine. Fuel passages in the carburettor are very small and it takes only a very small piece of dirt to block or even partially block them, almost certainly stopping the engine on the low throttle position or causing erratic running and power loss at full throttle.

Fuel filtering is essential, although there will always be so-called experts who claim that 'the only way to operate your engine reliably is to filter the fuel as you fill the tank'. Their reasoning is that adding the extra element to the fuel feed system in the form of a filter firstly provides two extra places for air leaks to occur (at each end of the filter where the fuel pipe is connected up) and if the filter does its job by filtering out dirt it can become blocked during flight.

I admire these 'experts'. They are far more careful and painstaking than I can ever hope to be. If you remember to wipe the fuel filler pipe before connecting it up, if you make absolutely certain that no trace of dirt finds its way onto the fuel filler outlet pipe before you hook up, and as long as your hands are also clean whilst you fill up and all your pieces of fuel tube and the entire tank is clean, then you will not suffer dirt problems. I maintain that the average modeller will find it easier to check fuel tubing for splits now and again and clean out a filter from time to time than remember the meticulous cleansing procedure required to end up with a tank of clean fuel. Accept that there will be a small amount of dirt in your fuel tank and keep it out of the carburettor with a good filter.

Which way up is the right way?

Strictly speaking the engine doesn't know which way up it is and if we don't tell it, it will run perfectly in any attitude! Joking aside, there is no theoretical reason why the engine should not be turned to whatever angle is convenient for the particular model. There are some practical problems that have to be faced whichever way up the engine is to be run, and first and foremost is the fuel tank position.

Most problems relating to engines run in an inverted position are due to the fuel tank not being sited correctly. Irrespective of the engine's positioning, the tank must be lined up with the carburettor correctly.

5 Starting and running

Pre-flight checks. Step by step start-up procedure. Golden rules for start-up. Use of rev counter for needle valve adjusting. Knocking, pinking and detonation; effects of compression ratio, fuel formulation, glow-plugs and propeller loading. Cures for detonation.

So far all mentions of running model four-strokes have painted a happy picture of smooth-running reliability, with engines starting virtually instantly and running smoothly until the user becomes bored with the whole operation, and they have conveniently glossed over some of the operational snags. It is likely that first experiences with a new modern engine will be happy ones, particularly if the wisdom of bench operation is appreciated and the opportunity taken to become familiar with the motor before it is installed in a model. Once out on the flying field the whole situation seems to change and it is at this point that a proper and familiar operating procedure will show its benefit.

Before you leave
Hardly pre-flight checks, the following should be thought of as essential daily checks that are carried out before the model even gets as far as the family transport that is to carry it to the flying field. Assuming that the model structure and R/C system have had their own maintenance checks, then the following is a suggested list of checks for the power plant – not actual maintenance, just checks to see that everything appears to be as it should be. Full maintenance will be covered elsewhere.

(a) Remove cowls if fitted.
(b) Remove glow-plug from engine and turn over as many times as necessary to expel all traces of preservative oil left in it. Ideally, spin over with an electric starter – if you do this, place a piece of rag over the glow-plug hole otherwise there will be oil all over the workshop!

(c) Re-fit the plug if it looks to be in good condition with a bright shiny element, otherwise replace with a new plug. An oxidised, grey-looking appearance to the element will cause the plug to run cooler and probably spoil tick-over and even cause misfiring at high RPM.

(d) Check compression. Poor compression may be a result of gummed-up valves or piston rings, particularly if you use a castor oil based fuel, or it may be incorrect tappet clearances. A small amount of fuel primed down the inlet will cure sticky valves and help to ease piston rings but deeper investigation will be needed to reveal the tappets. Also check plug washer and element seal, listening for bubbling air leaks.

(e) Check all engine bolts for security. A visual check is usually sufficient, as loose bolts are usually indicated by signs of oil leakage. If any are suspected of being loose it will usually be necessary to remove the engine from the model to tighten them properly and evenly.

(f) Physically check the mounting bolts, both engine to mount and engine mount to bulkhead if appropriate. Vibration levels are often high in four-stroke engines and bolts can loosen quite quickly.

(g) Examine all fuel feed, breather and fuel pressure tubing, looking particularly carefully at the carburettor nipple area and the fuel tank outlet pipe areas. A slight pull on the tube to stretch it will usually show up both holes and splits. If there is anywhere that the tubing contacts the engine also check this carefully. Any suspect tubing should be replaced.

(h) Dismantle and clean out the fuel filter.

(i) Examine the propeller hub for signs of crushing and check the blades carefully for any splits. Any damage to the propeller that is found indicates a need for immediate replacement.

(j) If the carburettor main needle valve is fitted with a ratchet device, check that it is holding the needle valve in position as it should.

(k) Check that the R/C connection to the throttle lever of the carburettor is sound and operate the throttle over its full range of movement to ensure that the servo does not become stalled at full throttle, full forward trim or throttle closed, trim down setting.

Replace the cowls and load up your model. If all the above checks are satisfactorily completed there is a good day's flying ahead.

Once out on the field with your model assembled the time has come for pre-flight checks proper and the start-up ritual, and it is a ritual. Carry it out methodically, use the same step approach on each

Filling the tank. Pumps, either manual or electric, are commonly used for the quantities required for radio flying.

and every occasion that you go flying and you will enjoy a lot more success than those who adopt a haphazard approach to their engines. When engines are reduced to model size they are also reduced to model simplicity and the casual climb in, switch on attitude that can be adopted towards the family car will just not work with the model engine. A lot of technology is required to make the switch-on and go philosophy work – just take a look at the carburettor in the family transport for confirmation. All the linkages and lumps are there to make the device automatic in start-up and running processes. Look at the ignition system, a little more complex than your model engine glow system, isn't it?

Technology makes the necessary steps for you in your family car. When you pull out the choke the throttle is opened to a precise degree, the thermostatically operated air control will already have set itself to the warm air position and as you turn on the ignition, the ballasted coil will be able to provide a full voltage spark even though the current drain of the starter turning over a cold engine is immense. That same ignition system will also automatically provide a spark at precisely the correct time to best ignite the richened mixture at the slow RPM of the electric starter's operation.

Every engine requires this same set of correct operating conditions if it is to start up reliably. In a model situation it is up to you, the operator, to provide them, as little or no technology is built in to the engine for you.

Proceed as follows:

(a) Fill up your fuel tank. Beware of allowing any model, irrespective of engine installation, to stand for a long while with full tanks. Fuel can syphon into the carburettor and flood the engine. If you can, a pinch-off device on the fuel feed pipe from tank to engine is a good idea. Suitable devices are available from model shops and many helicopter flyers use them.

(b) If the engine is fitted with a choke, close this and turn over the engine a few times with the throttle slightly open to draw fuel into the cylinder. Do not operate the choke while spinning the engine over with an electric starter, which could flood the engine. When the engine is turned over for choking, any resistance that could indicate that it is already flooded should be watched out for. If the engine does appear to be flooded, the safest route is to remove the glow-plug immediately and turn over the engine till it is clear. Replace the plug and check again for signs that it is not clear before proceeding.

(c) Connect up the glow battery and observe the meter, which should indicate that the plug is glowing and also give a 'normal' reading if, of course, you can remember what that should be! You should be able to feel a kick as the piston goes over top dead centre on the compression stroke, indicating that there is fuel present and it is being ignited by the glow-plug.

(d) If the vital signs are present, then with the throttle closed either flick or electric start your motor into life. If they are not, disconnect the plug and choke further, repeating until there is fuel present and the engine kicks when turned over. It may be necessary to open the throttle 2 or 3 clicks of the trim for cold starts.

(e) There is a possibility, particularly with tail-dragger style models, that the fuel draw may not be sufficient to pull the fuel up to the carburettor with the tail wheel on the ground. If you suspect this to be the case it will be necessary either to carry a block or box with you or get someone to hold the tail up for you until the motor is running. This is usually only a problem for the first start-up of the day and subsequent runs seem to present no problems.

(f) Before making adjustments or opening the throttle fully, move round to the rear of the propeller disc. NEVER stand in line with the propeller of a model engine. However slight,

59

there is always a risk that a blade may be thrown from the propeller.

The Golden Rules of starting up are quite simply:

Never turn over an engine with a starter until you have checked by hand.
Never electric start and choke simultaneously.
Never force an engine to turn over, it could be flooded with raw fuel.
Beware of the dangers of the propeller and never use a damaged propeller.
Always use a glow-plug battery with a meter.
Remember there must be Fuel, Compression and Ignition present if the engine is to run.

Setting up for flight

A valuable accessory for the real enthusiast is a rev counter. There are several types available but the best for modelling purposes is the optical sensing type with a digital reading. The exhaust note of the four-stroke does not allow of easy judgement of either maximum or minimum RPM. Correctness of full throttle mixture strength can be readily gauged if the RPM of the engine is monitored while the needle valve is adjusted. As the fuel mixture is weakened the RPM will be seen to rise, then flatten out and finally start to falter as the weakening mixture starts to overheat the engine and cause a loss of power. By observing the maximum RPM achieved and then richening the mixture enough to slow the engine 200–300 RPM a satisfactory setting should be arrived at.

As for the idle speed, the low exhaust noise level and the fact that the engine only fires once every 2 revolutions does make idle setting particularly difficult. A speed of around 2500 RPM should be achievable with most engines, and some will idle far more slowly than this. The engine tests in magazines give actual figures of some engines to give some idea of the lowest reliable idle obtained. The accent must be on reliability: the engine should be able to idle for at least 1 minute and ideally much more, yet still respond cleanly to opening of the throttle. Properly set up, there are few engines that will not turn in this type of figure.

Actual idle RPM are set by the throttle stop adjuster screw. Figure 20 illustrates the location on typical carburettors. Initially the idle speed should be set for around 3,000 RPM and then adjustments made to the idle mixture strength using the idle mixture control adjustment. There are several types of adjustment for idle mixture but Figures 12 & 13 in Chapter 3 show the most common. Chapter 3

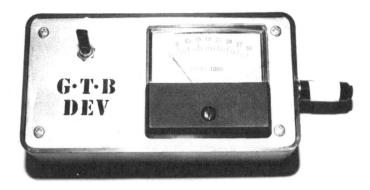

An optical tachometer. This one simply registers r.p.m. in 1000s and is very easy to use, though digital read-out is preferred by some.

also gives basic information on adjusting carburettors. Be prepared to persevere for some time, making very small adjustments and then observing the results. If all your efforts seem to make matters worse, then it is probably time to revert to square one by re-setting both the main needle valve and the idle mixture control needle valve.

A simple and basic method of doing this is firstly to attach a length of fuel tubing to the fuel inlet nipple, then set the main needle valve at the approximate running setting – about three turns open. Adjust the throttle stop screw to open the throttle about 0.5 mm and gently blow down the fuel tubing with the throttle closed. Adjust the idle mixture control needle until it is just possible to blow through the

Fig. 20

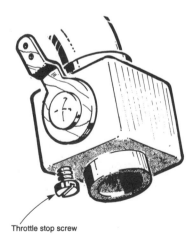

Throttle stop screw

61

carburettor. This ensures that with the main needle valve set and the throttle closed, fuel can still flow through into the engine. This method usually results in a setting that will allow the engine to run!

Remember, unless the engine is well run in, the idle performance may well be erratic. If the engine is not fully free, allow it to accumulate some more running time before attempting to finally set the idle mixture.

Leave it alone!

Once the idle mixture and main mixture are set properly it is very unlikely that they will ever need further adjustment unless the fuel type or propeller size or type is changed. It may well be that a change of model or enclosing the engine in a cowling will demand a change in setting even though the propeller and fuel stay the same. In general terms, the operating conditions that our model engines are exposed to are quite uniform. The atmospheric temperature range in which most modellers are prepared to fly is quite small, the atmospheric pressure range is also limited – both comments of course relate to possible extremes and those that could be coped with following adjustments are huge. Providing that the foregoing instructions referring to setting up of mixture are followed then the engine will be set a miniscule amount too rich on some days but a tiny mite too lean on others. In neither case would the result obtainable from messing about with the needle valves be detectable. If you doubt the wisdom of these comments ask yourself why there is no needle valve on your family car or the side of a jumbo jet?

If you do adopt this attitude there will be one very big benefit in that there will be an immediate indication of fuel feed problems that otherwise could not exist. The slightest blockage will be shown by hesitation in the engine's running. If the engine will not draw fuel

If it takes a few minutes to set an engine up take heart – the builder of this Junkers Ju52 had three to cope with!

62

unless the needle valve is opened it is a sure sign that something is blocked and a remedy can be sought before there is a disaster.

If you re-adjust the needle valve unnecessarily for each flight then you can never be sure whether the faulty running is a result of incorrect adjustment for that one flight or something more fundamental.

The ultra-cautious may well feel that some leeway to the 'leave-it-alone' philosophy should be granted. Well, if the weather is really hot, far hotter than that in which the engine was originally set up, then there is a case for richening the mixture before the flight. A one-eighth turn of the main needle valve is enough for most purposes and can be re-set to the proven norm as soon as the weather returns to its usual.

Knocking and backfiring

Some early commercially-produced four-strokes were very prone to both 'knocking' and 'backfiring', both inter-related problems and with some common causes. Tackling the knocking or detonation problem first, this is probably quite familiar to most car drivers where it is usually known as 'pinking'.

Pre-ignition is the cause of the tinny clicking noise that comes from the engine if it is asked to produce too much at too low an RPM. The actual controlled burning of fuel and air that occurs inside the cylinder of the engine is a complex result of the combined cylinder pressure, engine temperature, flash point of the fuel, timing of the ignition point and shape of the combustion chamber. Alter any one of the factors and the performance characteristics of the engine change.

If, for example, the mixture is too weak then the result will be a rise in cylinder temperature (less cooling effect from the incoming fuel and a higher temperature burn from the changed fuel/air mix) which causes a chain reaction-like build-up leading to earlier ignition point (higher cylinder temperature nearer to flashpoint of fuel, giving the classic pre-ignition symptoms) and knocking as the piston tries to continue its compression of gases which are by now burning and trying to expand! The resultant knocking can usually be heard quite clearly and is usually immediately cured by richening the fuel mixture.

Altering the degree of compression can also have a similar effect. It has been argued that too high an oil content in the fuel will effectively raise the compression ratio by taking up space in the combustion chamber and may thus cause knocking, but a few seconds' thought will make one realise that the actual volume of oil in each individual cylinder charge is pretty small, even when

63

considered as a percentage of the admittedly small combustion chamber volume. The more likely reason is not that the extra oil raises the compression ratio but that it improves the piston seal and improves efficiency, giving higher cylinder pressures which in turn gives rise to pre-ignition.

The above reason apart, too high an oil content is not a good idea, for not only does it seem to have a bad effect on running, it also messes up models and gives a very smoky exhaust and must also lead to a more rapid build up of internal carbon.

Excessive loads also badly affect the performance and lead to pre-ignition, this as a result of the fixed nature of the ignition timing provided by a glow-plug. What seems to happen is that the mixture strength and throttle opening are trying to tell the engine that it should be operating at one RPM whereas the load of the propeller is holding it back and the glow-plug tries to ignite the fuel mixture at a point appropriate to a higher RPM than is being achieved. Once again pre-ignition and a drop-off of performance result.

In a nutshell, mixture strength should never be weakened to the extent that a harshness of the exhaust note indicates pre-ignition, nor should fuels with too high an oil content be used or propeller loads be excessive. Once again an audible warning of problems will often be heard.

Taken to excess, the pre-ignition syndrome can be so bad that the engine just does not turn over dead centre. It fires so early that instead it rotates backwards, often throwing off the propeller in a classic backfire. This is usually the result of closing down the fuel needle to too weak a setting.

Refitting the propeller and richening the mixture is more often than not all that is required for a cure. However, if the engine is very new, the cause is likely to be the very good fit between piston and cylinder already described and the problem will only reduce as the engine is run in. The early Enya 35-4c engine suffered from this problem, largely due to its Aluminium Piston, Chrome Plated Brass

Locking nuts with a fibre or plastic insert help to prevent propellers loosening with backfiring.

(ABC) cylinder assembly. This type of construction requires a very close-fitting piston to start with and relies on the expansion of the cylinder to give clearance when the engine is hot. The situation was seemingly caused by the cooling period of the exhaust and induction strokes of the four-stroke cycle which caused the cylinder to contract and pinch the piston more closely than when it was warm. Result, an engine that backfired at every possible chance and took several hours to run in. Enya no longer use the ABC system for four-strokes.

Persistent problems with prop loosening can be if not cured then at least prevented from causing undue frustration by one of the following methods:

(a) Application of a thread locking compound to the crankshaft threads. This will not stop the nut from coming undone but will stop the nut from flying off into the long grass!

(b) A Nylock style nut, the British made 'Laser' engines are supplied with such a nut.

(c) Wrap some cotton into the bottom of the crankshaft threads to act in the same way as thread locking compound.

(d) Use a second nut as a lock or jam nut.

Once the engine has been fully run in, if the problems persist firstly try changing to a four-stroke formula fuel. The lower oil content in this may well give a cure. Try also the effect of reducing the propeller pitch by an inch, which may reduce the load to the extent that the problem goes away. If all else fails then the only remaining solutions are to try different glow-plugs or lower the compression ratio. Plug changes can sometimes work but the probable result of finding a plug that stops pre-ignition will be to spoil the tick-over.

Reducing the compression ratio is quite a simple operation providing that your engine uses a cylinder head gasket or, if it has a fixed cylinder head as on latest Saitos, a gasket between the cylinder and crankcase. If a gasket is fitted, quite simply obtain a second gasket and fit two. This will increase the squish band clearance and lower the compression ratio. With metal gaskets there is no reason why even more gaskets should not be fitted. If you have a rev counter it is a simple task to optimise the number of gaskets by observing the RPM as successive gaskets are fitted and going back one step as soon as a drop-off in performance is noted. Remember that each time you change a gasket on a pushrod operated overhead valve engine you will have to re-adjust the tappets.

6 Fuels and plugs

Fuel formulation, basic constituents and their effects. Methanol, oil types and characteristics. Nitro-methane. Mixtures for castor and synthetic oil fuels. Advantages and disadvantages of using Nitro-methane. Corrosion inhibitors. Commercial fuels. Glow-plugs, how they work. 'Hot' or 'Cold' plugs. Maintenance.

Model four-strokes are by and large designed to run on a mixture of methyl alcohol (methanol) and oil with the addition of small proportions of Nitro-methane (nitro) in most instances. Methanol provides the actual fuel in the main, although the calorific value of the burning of the small quantities of oil present cannot be ignored, nor can its effect on the happenings within the combustion chamber.

The actual oil used depends on several factors, firstly on its ability to mix with the methanol. The two types that mix readily with methanol are castor oil, a vegetable product with extraordinarily good properties of lubrication under the extreme conditions prevailing within a model engine and, secondly, finding much favour with modellers are the 'synthetic' oils. These latter oils are chemically or biologically 'engineered' lubricants that have most of the desirable qualities of castor oil plus some additions. To help with an understanding of the effects of varying proportions of ingredients, the actions of those ingredients during the four-stroke cycle should be understood.

Methanol
The choice of methanol for the energy releasing element of the fuel for model engines is directly a result of the very simple form of ignition chosen. Earlier model engines duplicated the full-size engine spark ignition systems, but the need to carry coil, condenser, contact breaker, battery and associated wiring persuaded weight-conscious modellers to seek alternatives. In Europe, the alternative first to find popular appeal was the compression ignition or so-called 'diesel' whereas the glow ignition system attracted the American

66

modeller. Unfortunately glow ignition and petrol do not go together, as the glow-plug temperature is really inadequate for reliable ignition of the petrol and, in any event, if the plug is hot enough, the petrol will be ignited by the glow-plug far too early in the cycle, causing pre-ignition and knocking. Alcohol on the other hand is a slower burning fuel and can tolerate the very advanced ignition point that is a characteristic of the glow system. This means that even at the high compression ratios that would worsen the pre-ignition tendency if petrol were to be used, but are so important for good performance, methanol still burns in a controllable manner without pre-igniting. It is interesting to note that for many years alcohol was used as an 'anti-knock' agent in fuels, along with naphthalene, only to be replaced with tetra ethyl lead. Some readers will probably remember the Discol brand of petrol which had a high proportion of alcohol.

It may well be that the small water content of the commercial grades of methanol used for fuels is also of benefit. Water injection is used on large diesel engines to smooth the running and provide better performance by slowing the rate of burning and also producing steam which continues to exert an expansive force on the piston after the effect of the fuel burn has started to diminish. The cooling effect of the methanol is also beneficial: air-cooled engines

Four-strokes have advanced so much in a matter of four or five years that it is quite normal to fit one in a scale aerobatic model.

intended for running on methanol fuel can use smaller areas of cooling fins and save on weight. Nor should the safety aspect be disregarded. Methanol needs more than a spark to ignite it in normal circumstances, but petrol is very easy to ignite and flying site fuel spillages where petrol is concerned can represent a real danger.

Lubricating oil
The purpose of the lubricating oil is two-fold. Firstly it keeps the moving parts from actual contact with one another by forming a thin and tenacious film between them. The ability of the oil to hold together under high pressure and high temperature is crucial. Castor oil has this ability in abundance and will usually continue to provide lubrication even after the best of synthetics has broken down.

Transfer of heat away from the bearing area is of almost equal importance, and in full size practice engines that are subject to continuous high stress are almost always fitted with some means of keeping the oil cool. In model engines where the oil is used on a total loss basis this cooling of recirculated oil does not occur.

Nitro-methane
Nitro-methane is a complex compound, high in oxygen, that is added to the fuel as a power improver. When it is heated, as in an internal combustion engine chamber, the oxygen is released to aid the combustion process. This additional oxygen release demands additional fuel (methanol) to burn with it and the most obvious result of adding more nitro to fuel (apart from the extra power output) is the need to re-adjust the fuel mixture control needle to a richer (more fuel) setting.

Nitro is only used in very small percentages in four-stroke engines, typically 5-10%. Adding greater percentages is a very costly business and does not reward the user with corresponding increases in power.

Fuel formulations
A classic blend that will allow most engines to run is:

Methanol   – 80%
Oil   – 20%

For most purposes the oil content for four-stroke fuel could be reduced to 16% (or 6 parts methanol to 1 part oil) when using castor oil, with complete safety; some engine manufacturers allow for an even lower castor oil content. If synthetic oils of the type intended for gas turbine lubrication are used, this percentage can be lowered

68

even further, to as low as 5%. I would not recommend that such a low percentage be used for practical purposes, as the actual amount of oil entering the engine as a constituent of the fuel is very small in this situation and a very slight maladjustment of the carburettor towards the weak mixture side will result in inadequate lubrication.

A safe formulation for pure synthetic oil fuel would be:

Methanol	– 88%
Synthetic oil	– 12%

But by far the best and safest approach when using synthetic oils would be to supplement the synthetic with a small proportion of castor oil, giving a formulation of:

Methanol	– 88%
Synthetic oil	– 8%
Castor oil	– 4%

Using this formulation the benefits of using synthetic oil will still be noticed whilst the safety of castor will still be present.

It would not be unreasonable to question the reasons for using synthetic oils at all if there is an element of doubt surrounding their practicality. As far as the user is concerned the benefits will be, firstly, none of the 'gumming up' associated with castor oil, which solidifies inside the engine between runs, making the engine very stiff to turn over after it has stood for some time. If the engine is left for very long periods the castor oil can actually solidify, forming a layer over moving parts and often causing irreparable damage to parts such as ball-races when the engine is started up, unless the residue is flushed from the engine beforehand. Piston rings also suffer, becoming gummed into their grooves and unable to spring out against the cylinder walls to provide a good seal for starting compression.

By contrast, an engine running on synthetic oil fuel will always be relatively free, even after long periods of inaction, remaining easy to start with good compression. An added benefit is the absence of the very sticky residue that is sprayed all over the model as the engine is run. Because there is less oil anyway this is reduced and that which is present is very much easier to remove. Finally, fuel consumption by volume is reduced as more of the fuel is actually combustible, i.e. there is more methanol present per cc.

As discussed in Chapter 2, as a total exception to the rule, the manufacturers of the Swedish Damo horizontally opposed twin cylinder four-stroke of 1.10 cu.in. (18 cc) capacity recommend a fuel that contains No Oil. The methanol itself has slight lubricating qualities and it has proved practical to operate these engines as advised. The safe operation is helped by the use of roller bearings for the connecting rod and users will have to apply some oil to such items as valve rockers, crankshaft bearings, cams, etc., from time to time.

Although some manufacturers recommend that no nitro should be used in their products (notably AGC Engineering, manufacturers of the British 'Laser' range) most do advise small quantities. Use of nitro is a double-edged sword for while it is certainly true that by adding nitro to fuel both the performance in terms of power output and the flexibility and starting of the engine will be improved, it is certain that its addition adds considerably to the risks of internal corrosion of the engine.

There are many well-documented cases of four-stroke engines being ruined in very short time by internal corrosion. The model four-stroke relies on leakage of oil past the piston for lubrication of the crankshaft, cams, gears and connecting rod and with the oil that reaches the crankcase there is inevitably going to be a proportion of burnt fuel residue. Once this condenses in the crankcase it tends to become trapped after the engine is stopped. Even though there is a breather present, this is only really effective whilst the engine is running, and in between the operating sessions the condensed fluids will attack the exposed metal parts, wreaking havoc.

Nitro adds to this corrosion problem considerably, turning the condensate in the crankcase to nitric acid. The more nitro, the worse the problem is likely to be. If nitro-bearing fuels are to be used, it is imperative that the operator be aware of the results of neglect and take positive action to prevent damage.

However, to my mind the benefits outweigh the disadvantages for the following reasons:

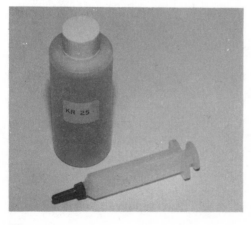

A plastic syringe is supplied with this brand of corrosion inhibitor to be used for mixing or post-run application.

(a) Particularly in cold weather, the engine will be easier to start and will run more consistently. In very cold weather the engine may not run at all without the glow-plug connected without nitro.

(b) The carburettor becomes significantly easier to adjust. Once again cold weather adds to the difficulty of achieving a good idle without the nitro present.

(c) The engine will need a richer mixture setting with nitro fuel, meaning that a higher volume of oil and cooling methanol flows through the engine.

(d) It is possible to run the engine with a richer than optimum mixture setting and still experience the same output power because of the power-enhancing effect of the nitro, meaning once again more safety margin against a too-weak setting. This can often be the difference between the engine quitting as the model nose is raised during climb-out and it continuing to pull well.

Overall, I would consider the benefits not to be of power improvement, but of operational flexibility and reliability.

Corrosion inhibitors
One means of preventing corrosion is by coating parts liable to corrosion with a barrier layer of corrosion-inhibiting oil. Such oils are readily available and undoubtedly work in the right situations. Unhappily, their performance in corrosion prevention when used in model four-strokes has not proved to be the total answer when added to the fuel. It is not that the oils do not work but more that their ability to remain in place in the environment of the engine crankcase is not good enough, coupled with the fact that the very low volume that can find its way to the place where it is needed is not sufficient. Only very low volumes of corrosion-inhibiting oils can be added to the fuel before it detracts from the performance and, because it is mixed with the fuel, a percentage of that that is there will be burnt anyway.

The lazy man's answer is not then good enough! Such oils must be applied to the engine after the day's running has been completed, when they will perform as required, displacing corrosive fluids from metal parts and forming the anti-corrosive barrier desired. Several such oils are widely available as 'Lay-up Oil', 'After-run Treatment' etc. If they are not to be found, a good quality machine oil will do almost as well.

Commercial fuels
Almost every model shop in the country will have in stock a variety of ready-to-use fuel varying from national brand-named blends to their

own local brew. When buying fuels in the first instance try to find a fuel that is recommended for use with four-strokes. Such a fuel will almost certainly have a lower oil content than that intended for use with two-strokes and will be beneficial for the reasons outlined above. You will usually find a choice between castor and synthetic fuels but in some instances the prejudice of the 'more mature' modeller will show and it may be difficult to find synthetic oil-based fuels. Make up your own mind from the data given here and if you can't find what you want straight away, persevere, the search will be worth it. Any commercial fuel with 'straight' or no-nitro formulation will do, but ideally look for 5% nitro. Look after your fuel once you have it. Always keep the container sealed when you are not actually fuelling up your model and remember that it is very inflammable. Keep containers out of the sun, since the evaporation of the fuel inside a sealed container can build up a high pressure and in such situations if the container falls over serious leakages can occur. You may also find that fuel exposed to the sun for long periods becomes badly discoloured and spillages on your model may result in stains.

Beware of excessive direct skin contact with methanol, it is absorbed through the skin and the human metabolism finds it difficult to purge from the system. Be particularly careful not to get fuel in your eyes, the nitro is very bad for them as well as being painful. Lots of clean water should be used to flush out the eyes if you do have an accident.

Glow-plugs

At a first glance, the glow-plug is deceptively simple, just a coil of silvery wire housed in a simple machined metal screwed plug with provision for connecting each end of the coil to a source of electrical power for heating purposes. Over the years my own conception of the glow-plug has steadily modified from this simplistic view as my questioning regarded quirks of performance of model engines has demanded answers.

The fuel used in model four-strokes when compressed at the common compression ratios found (between 7.5–8.5:1) will not spontaneously ignite. There has to be some additional heat input. A true diesel engine operates at something in excess of 16.5:1 and requires no ignition other than the heat generated by compression. In our present case the additional heat is supplied by an incandescent element, usually in the form of a coil in the glow-plug placed in the cylinder head. Materials used for the elements vary considerably, containing various proportions of Platinum, Iridium and Rhodium, all of which come under the generic term Precious Metals. Platinum is a particularly interesting element which can act

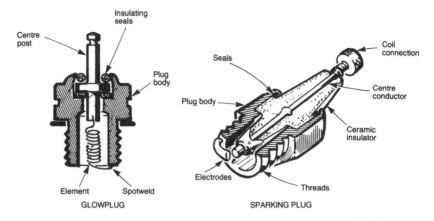

Fig. 21

as a catalyst in many chemical reactions, including the model engine combustion chamber where it causes heat to be generated when it comes into contact with the inflammable gases present.

Straight away there is an interesting situation, for not only does the electrical heating of the element have a bearing but so does this catalytic reaction. When the engine is cold and in a starting situation, catalytic heating is not sufficient to allow the engine to fire and a booster battery is essential. Once the engine is running, a combination of catalytic reaction and heat retention between firing strokes keeps sufficient heat in the plug for continuous running without electrical boost. See Figure 21.

The actual point at which the mixture within the combustion chamber is ignited in relation to the position of the piston up and down the cylinder is critical to the smoothness and power of the engine. It is normal to arrange for the fuel to be ignited well before the piston reaches the top of its travel (TDC) so that the flame can spread evenly throughout the combustion chamber and be efficiently burning and expanding as the piston travels downwards again. In a spark ignition engine this ignition point is precisely controlled by a contact breaker which is able to vary the ignition point in response to the rotational speed of the engine.

A glow-plug, however, is glowing all the time and the sole control over actual ignition point is that of temperature of the element which will at a given temperature ignite the gas as it reaches a certain degree of compression. The hotter the element, the earlier the gas will be ignited in the compression stroke – in other words, the more *advanced* will be the ignition. As the glow-plug has to retain its heat during an exhaust stroke glow-plugs for four-strokes will almost

73

certainly have to have high heat retention capabilities as compared with a plug for a two-stroke. They will be 'hot' plugs. The temperature retention ability of the plug is governed by the material thickness of the element, the size of the cavity in which it is housed and its position within the combustion chamber.

The alloy used will also have a bearing as the catalytic effect can be either increased or reduced depending on constituent proportions.

Fortunately for the user of the model four-stroke all the work of developing and selecting glow-plugs is usually done for us by the engine manufacturer in conjunction with the glow-plug manufacturer. All we need do is fit what is recommended. However, it is always possible that by virtue of the fuel chosen or the altitude or temperature prevailing that the plug recommended does not work very well. Choosing an alternative is a difficult business. If the engine consistently quits on idle it is likely that the plug chosen is too 'cold', meaning that there is insufficient heat retention to keep the fire going from one firing stroke to the next. Too hot a plug will often cause detonation: the ignition point will be too far advanced and the burn will be in a very advanced state before the piston reaches TDC, causing overheating and a harsh note to the exhaust. Most manufacturers rate their plugs as 'Hot', 'Standard' or 'Cold' and so it should be possible to experiment in a controlled fashion. Unhappily there is no absolute standard for temperature ratings so it may well be that one manufacturer's 'hot' plug equates to another's 'standard'. If it so happens that fitting a hotter plug to an engine that won't idle properly causes detonation, try the interim step of fitting a shielded

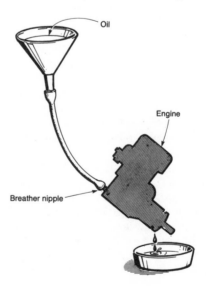

Fig. 22

74

or 'R/C' type of plug. This type of plug is really intended for two-stroke motors where the fuel enters the combustion chamber in an upward direction towards the plug which can thus be doused. However, in an overhead valve four-stroke the incoming fuel is entering in a downward direction relative to the plug and the shield or 'idle bar' is not normally considered necessary. Such plugs are sometimes the only way of assuring reliable ignition with inverted engine installations.

If all else fails, use a booster circuit operated via a micro-switch closed as the throttle servo travels to the low throttle position. A comparatively small nicad fast rechargeable cell can be used: 1.2 Ampere Hour will provide more than a day's flying. A switch must be fitted otherwise the plug will be continuously energised all the while the throttle is closed, with the possibility of the engine being inadvertently started while being turned over.

Maintenance

Already in this chapter there has been mention of the need to protect the engine between operating sessions. Approach this chore in a thorough fashion and not only will the engine itself benefit, but there will almost certainly be a bonus of more enjoyable general operation, for it is surprising how often other faults will be discovered as the protective routine is carried out.

As soon as the flying session is over drain the fuel tank and, if the engine is cowled in, remove the cowls. Thoroughly clean up the exterior of the engine with a strong detergent solution. Be particularly careful to remove all traces of grit from around the glow-plug, otherwise during the next stage of the operation it may find its way into the engine.

Take out the glow-plug, find a length of fuel tube with which to connect an oil can to the breather and while holding the model nose down, squirt oil into the crankcase via the breather, meanwhile turning the engine over to distribute the oil thoroughly. See Figure 22.

Now squirt oil through the glow-plug hole and down the carburettor intake, turning over the engine to spread the oil thoroughly. Replace the plug very loosely; just sufficient threads should be engaged to retain it and keep dirt and moisture from entering the engine.

The truly provident will wrap the engine in an oily rag at this point and keep the cowls off until the next flying session. Before taking the model out, remove the rag, remove the glow-plug and spin the engine over with your starter until all the protecting oil has been expelled. Examine the element of the plug before replacing, it should have a bright clean appearance without any sign of pitting. Even if the plug glows when connected up it will need to be replaced from time to time, as surface corrosion and oxidation will impair its efficiency and cause erratic running. Replace the glow-plug and very carefully turn over the engine by hand. Any hint of excessive compression will mean that there is still oil trapped in the combustion chamber and the plug should be removed and the oil expelled.

Adjusting the tappets
From time to time the clearances between the end of the valve stem and the valve rockers (tappets) should be adjusted. On most modern engines this will require removal of the rocker cover. Refer to the engine instruction manual for the clearance required. Most model engine tappets will require cold adjustment and before making the adjustment it is advisable to tighten the cylinder head fixing bolts. In the case of the latest Saito engines, for head bolts read cylinder fixing bolts, as these engines have their cylinder head integral with the cylinder.

The feeler gauge is slipped between the rocker and the valve stem and is best kept straight rather than curved as in this photo, to get a more accurate 'pinch'.

Fig. 23

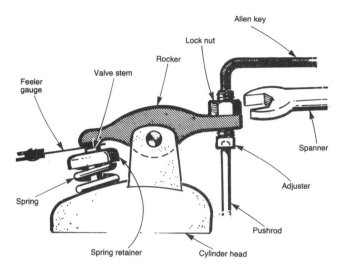

Most engines are supplied with a feeler gauge for adjusting the tappets, but if not it is essential that you obtain one of the correct size. Always use tools that fit properly. A screwdriver or allen key and a small spanner for the locking nut will be needed – do not use pliers! Loosen the locknut, turn the engine over until the inlet valve opens, then closes fully. Continue to turn the engine for a half-revolution after the valve has closed to ensure that the cam follower is on the rear of the cam and the valve clearance is at a maximum. Slide the feeler gauge into the gap between rocker and valve and adjust until the feeler is just pinched. Tighten the locknut and re-check. You will almost certainly find that the clearance has opened out a little but by doing the job as described you will get a feel for the amount of 'pinch' required on the feeler. Repeat the operation for the exhaust valve. See Figure 23.

Turn the engine over carefully and if there is any indication that something is going to touch inside the engine re-check your work. If the engine turns over but has no compression, the clearance is insufficient or non-existent. Re-set the clearances. Replace the rocker cover and check again. You are now ready to start up.

7 Servicing

Servicing your engine. Some likely faults. Correct tools. Cylinder head removal. Cleaning the parts. Valve removal and grinding in. Piston and cylinder faults – removal. Fitting piston rings. Crankshaft and main bearing removal and replacement. Re-assembly and adjustment. Fault finding chart.

Although previous chapters have covered the most basic maintenance needs of the four-stroke, such as pre-running checks, after running checks and tappet adjustment, there will be other maintenance needs that will occur from time to time. The most important principle to be observed is 'leave well alone'. By all means check for signs of imminent trouble but do not take things to pieces for the sake of it.

Unless you are properly qualified by virtue of skill, experience, knowledge and wealth, do not attempt to take your engine to pieces. I say wealth advisedly, for you will always have to be prepared to replace parts that may be damaged by careless handling if you take the engine to pieces. Cost, or probable cost, is always a factor in maintenance. If you have not the ability or confidence then the only course that makes sense is to send the engine back to its manufacturer or their agents, which will cost money, but if you choose to do the job yourself, parts needed as a result of errors also cost money.

Signs of trouble or imminent trouble usually take one of the following forms:

(a) Poor idling performance or total inability to idle.
(b) Low compression and difficulty in starting.
(c) Mechanical noises.
(d) Difficulty in turning over the engine.
(e) Leakage of gases or oil from joints between parts.
(f) Excessive vibration.
(g) Very poor fuel draw.

Diagnosis of the root cause of most of the above problems can usually be achieved by the experienced operator without the need to dismantle the engine, but for many owners the answer can only be found after removing parts of the engine.

Tools for the job

Before embarking on any work on your engine make sure that you have the right tools for the job. Many four-strokes are supplied with suitable hexagon wrenches (allen keys) and spanners. If not you must obtain correctly fitting examples, plus new Phillips screwdrivers and correctly sharpened plain screwdrivers to fit the full range of screw sizes on your engine. Small pliers with 'snipe' and 'thin flat' noses of around 5 inch size will also be needed, as will a pair of tweezers, a plug spanner, a wooden dowel, a few blocks of wood, a tray to contain the parts, solvent for cleaning and a supply of rags and kitchen paper for cleaning. During reassembly you will need a good quality machine oil to lubricate the parts.

Before starting to dismantle your pride and joy there are one or two things you can do to help analyse the likely cause of trouble. If poor compression is suspected (symptoms are (a) and (g) above) then try removing the carburettor and exhaust pipes and turning the engine over while listening carefully to the inlet and exhaust ports. You may be able to hear air leaking from the valves as the engine compresses the gas in the cylinder. You could even place the engine under water and look for air bubbles escaping from the ports as the engine is turned over.

By grasping the crankcase securely and applying sideways pressure to the crankshaft via the propeller and turning, badly worn crankshaft ballraces will often be indicated by a roughness or gritty feeling as the shaft is turned. In extreme cases, it may be possible to detect movement in the races as the shaft is rocked by the propeller. Faulty bearings may also be a source of noise and oil leakages, both indications that renewal is needed. Once a basic diagnosis has been made, the next stage is dismantling.

Removing the cylinder head

Although this can be done with the engine installed in the model, this is not to be recommended. Remove the engine and thoroughly clean the outside. I use a stiff brush and strong detergent, washing the engine under the full force of the kitchen hot water tap. Now that the outside of the engine is spotless, your hands are probably dirty, so it is essential that you wash your hands before proceeding, otherwise dirt will be transferred to the parts of the engine as they are handled. If you are in any doubt as to your ability to remember how parts are to be put back together, take written notes and draw simple sketches as you proceed.

It may be necessary to remove the carburettor if this has a steadying fixing to the lower engine crankcase, but otherwise it is usually a simple matter of removing up to six screws to remove the head. It is always a good idea to label pushrods if they are external so that front or rear, left or right can be replaced in the same position as they first occupied. On engines using a belt drive rotary valve the recommended technique is somewhat more complicated.

Remove the belt cover if one is fitted and turn the engine over until the piston approaches top dead centre on the compression stroke. Remove the glow-plug and rock the camshaft back and forth until TDC is properly established. Make a tiny mark on the drive belt pulley and a convenient fixed part of the engine to enable the valve to be set up correctly again once the engine is reassembled. If such marks are made by the manufacturer they are usually detailed in the instructions and it will not of course be necessary for you to make any. Make sure the marks are observed carefully.

With the bolts removed it is usual for the head to simply lift off. If it is reluctant, turn over the engine carefully and compression will almost certainly lift it. If it still will not budge, make sure that you have removed all the screws, there may be a screw concealed beneath the valve rockers! A little oil in the combustion chamber can help if the head is still reluctant. On the latest Saito engines the cylinder head is integral with the cylinder barrel and top end maintenance is likely to be tricky for even the most experienced. The

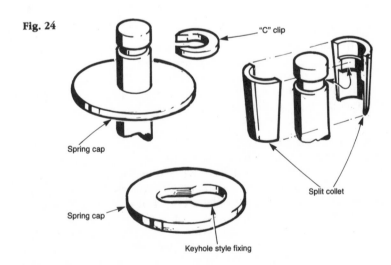

Fig. 24

"C" clip

Spring cap

Split collet

Spring cap

Keyhole style fixing

whole of the cylinder will come off with the head, exposing the piston and connecting rod assembly.

Although it is unlikely that valve seat leakages will cause poor compression, there is always the possibility and if this is indeed the case re-grinding the valves is a very simple way to restore the engine to its former performance. The valves will first have to be removed and this is done by compressing the valve springs away from the cotter that retains the valve spring cap. There are two types of spring retaining device commonly used, the 'C' shaped cap favoured by OS and the split collet used by Enya. See Figure 24. The split collet is tricky to fit: ideally, remove and refit inside a clear polythene bag, if bits fly in all directions at least they will remain in the bag!

Remove everything from the cylinder head and place the valve back in the head. Lift the valve a small way from the seat and apply a tiny dab of very fine grinding paste to the contact area and rotate the valve back and forth against the seat. If the valve has a slot in it use a screwdriver twirled between the fingers to rotate the valve. If not, I use a pencil with a rubber fixed to it to apply the necessary turning force. Only slight pressure is needed. When the seat and valve both have a uniform smooth appearance the grinding operation is complete. Every trace of the grinding paste must now be removed before the head is reassembled. A wash in strong solvent such as petrol or methylated spirits using a clean container with fresh fluid for a final wash should suffice. Apply a small quantity of oil to the valve stem as it is fitted.

Digging deeper

The most likely cause of poor compression is a worn piston and cylinder. On engines with front-mounted crankshafts such as the OS and Saito products the piston and cylinder can be removed quite easily after taking off the cylinder head and removing the backplate.

Pushing out the cylinder liner with a dowel. Do not use a metal rod for such operations.

Mark the connecting rod before removal with a pencil or felt pen to ensure same-way replacement.

This should enable the cylinder liner to be drawn up through the crankcase. A push upwards on the bottom edge of the liner with a wooden dowel is usually enough to push the liner up through the crankcase, but if it is reluctant warming up the case in a domestic oven will expand the crankcase and loosen the fit of the liner. On some engines there is a locking screw fitted to prevent the liner rotating in the crankcase and this will have to be removed before the liner can be withdrawn. This will usually be found on the rear side of the crankcase just below the cylinder cooling fins.

Once the liner is out, mark the exposed face of the connecting rod with a pencil so that it can be replaced in the same orientation. Turn the crankshaft until the piston is at bottom dead centre and lift the connecting rod off the crankpin with tweezers to allow the piston and connecting rod to drop out of the case.

Rather than fitting a complete piston and cylinder it is usually sufficient to fit a new ring the first time the engine loses

Support the crankcase (or front cover if separate) on wood blocks or soft vice clams before tapping out the crankshaft.

compression. Removing the old ring is easy, as it doesn't matter if it gets broken! Fitting the new is a delicate job as the rings are made from brittle cast iron. Over-stressing the ring will surely break it. Thoroughly clean out the groove in the piston before fitting the new ring. Lay the new ring on top of the piston and carefully spring one of the free ends down over the rim of the piston, gradually easing the remainder of the ring onto the piston. Once the whole ring is over the piston slide it down until it clicks into place in its groove.

Do check the fit of the gudgeon pin. If there is any slop in the bosses where the pin runs you will have to replace both piston and cylinder. Big end wear can also be assessed at this point; any detectable movement means that replacement of the connecting rod is required.

While the piston and rod are out, slide out the crankshaft and examine the bearings. This is simple on engines with rear mounted camshafts but will demand removal of the cam and cam followers on front mounted camshaft engines. Remove the camshaft after taking off the cover plate and withdrawing the cam followers. A sharp tap on the end of the crankshaft with a block of wood should release the collet that holds the propeller driver and allow the crank to drop out through the bearings. The ballraces should rotate with no sign of roughness or sideways play. The balls should not show any signs of corrosion or pitting, otherwise replacement is needed. Heat is certain to be necessary to release the ballraces from the crankcase. Place the case in a domestic oven set at 100-150°C for 5-10 minutes, then remove and sharply tap the complete case on a block of wood and the rear bearing should drop out. Repeat the operation for the front bearing. To replace the bearings, heat the case alone and place the bearing on the crankshaft and use this as an alignment mandrel to slide the new ballrace squarely into its housing. With the case still

The ball-races will slip out quite easily with the crankcase or cover heated. Hold in a thick cloth and tap sharply on wood.

Position the rear bearing first (left) and insert the front one subsequently. Crankshaft is used to ensure true alignment. Cold races slide easily into heated crankcase.

warm, slide the new front ballrace along the crankshaft into its housing. Do make certain that the ballraces are pushed really firmly into their housings.

The camshaft will be marked with a dot so that it can be properly aligned with the crankshaft gear. This stage must be right otherwise the valve timing will be incorrect and, at the very least, the engine will run very badly. The instructions usually include details of the timing marks and their application to reassembly.

Timing marks are fairly unobtrusive but should be found and lined up carefully for reassembly. Check valve operation carefully before attempting to run.

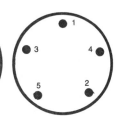

Fig. 25   Fig. 26

Lightly oil the bearings on the crankpin and gudgeon pin and drop the piston and rod down through the top of the case. Lift the rod onto the crankpin, remembering to take note of the marks placed on the rod when dismantling, and slide the cylinder liner into the top of the case. It is usually possible to compress the piston rings using a chamfer provided in the bottom edge of the cylinder liner. Slide the liner fully home and oil lightly and if a locking screw is fitted, replace this. Replace the backplate, tightening the screws as shown in Figure 25 to avoid the possibility of distorting the casting.

If pushrod cover tubes are used it will be necessary to fit these and the pushrods before the cylinder head is bolted into place. Tighten the head screws in the orders shown in Figure 26. Re-fit the propeller driver and carefully turn over the engine, feeling for any signs of tightness or internal collisions between parts which could indicate that the valve gear replacement has not been correctly carried out. Adjust the tappets, re-fit the carburettor and exhaust pipes and you are ready to run again.

Fault diagnosis

Problems	Possible Reasons	Remedies
Engine will not start (a) Engine has compression	Fuel tank empty	Replenish fuel supply
	Glow-plug not glowing	Check state of booster battery, check state of plug
	Fuel won't draw to carburettor	Open needle valve Check manifold sealing 'O' ring if fitted Examine fuel tubes for holes or splits

85

Problems	Possible Reasons	Remedies
(b) Engine has poor compression	Cylinder head screws loose	Tighten in accordance with Figure 25, Chapter 7
	Valve seats worn	Re-grind valves
	Piston/cylinder fit poor	Fit new piston ring or new piston/cylinder
	Glow-plug seal leaking	Fit new plug
	Glow-plug not seated	Clean plug and seating ' fit new washer
Engine runs harshly	Detonation	Richen fuel mixture. Use a lower pitch or larger diameter propeller. Fit an extra head gasket. Fit a 'cooler' plug
Engine throws off prop	Detonation	See above
	Not fully run-in	Run in for longer
Engine will not idle	Not fully run-in	Run in for longer
	Carburettor needs adjusting	Refer to Chapter 3
	Piston/cylinder fit poor	Replace parts
	Incorrect plug type	Fit recommended plug
	Idle speed set too low	Adjust throttle stop
Engine has low power	Poor compression	See above
	Mixture too weak/rich	See Chapter 3
	Incorrect fuel	See Chapter 6
	Incorrect propeller	See Manufacturer's recommendations
Engine overheats	Incorrect propeller	See above
	Incorrect mixture	See above
	Incorrect fuel	See above

Increasing power 8

*Towards higher performance. Combustion chamber design, cams
and ports. Super-charging and Turbo-charging. Temperature.
Tuned exhaust systems. Spark ignition by coil and magneto.
Ignition timing. Dangers of petrol fuels. Conclusion.*

Previous chapters have discussed the performance levels to be
expected from four-strokes and indicated that the lower power
output of current engines when compared with two-strokes of
equivalent capacity may not be expected to continue as
development proceeds. There are numerous ways of increasing
power outputs and more potent fuels might be thought a simple
example. Addition of nitro to the fuel used will increase the power
output but as has been shown there are disadvantages, and with four-
stroke engines operating at modest RPM levels, the effects are not as
marked as they would be in a two-stroke.

More likely areas of development are in combustion chamber
design, compression ratio increases and cam profiles. The power
output of the engine is to a large extent related to its efficiency as a
pump, and the cylinder's ability to draw in greater amounts of fuel,
compress it to a higher degree and then burn it effectively determine
the power. By running the engine faster the amount of fuel being
burnt in the cylinder ought to produce more power but as has been
described, raising the compression ratio can lead to an increased
tendency to pre-ignite, negating the attempt to raise the power.

Good combustion chamber design can help here by ensuring that
the flame can spread through the compressed gas as effectively and
quickly as possible. If the gas is swirling vigorously it helps and a
technique used to promote this swirling action is by use of a squish
area or band. See Figure 27. Careful positioning of the valves is also
needed so that the shape and smoothness of the combustion
chamber is not spoilt. The wedge-shaped combustion chamber
combined with a squish band drives the gases across the plug,
speeding up the ignition. As an incidental, one of the reasons why the

87

side valve engine does not perform as well as its overhead valve cousin is that the pocket to the side of the combustion chamber that houses the valves forms a dead area where the gas is difficult to ignite and also adds considerably to the combustion chamber volume, making it difficult to achieve high compression ratios.

Fig. 27

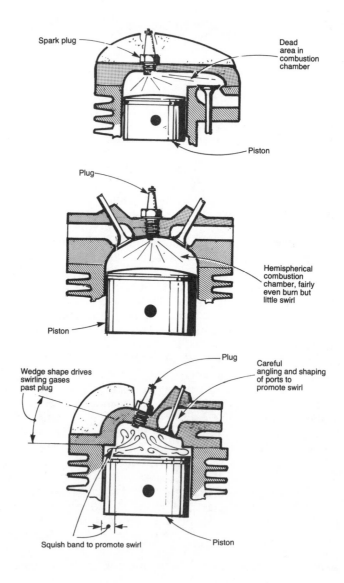

Spark plug

Dead area in combustion chamber

Piston

Plug

Hemispherical combustion chamber, fairly even burn but little swirl

Piston

Plug

Careful angling and shaping of ports to promote swirl

Wedge shape drives swirling gases past plug

Squish band to promote swirl

Piston

High compression ratios inevitably mean that the combustion chamber size with the piston at top dead centre is very small and very good control over poppet valves is needed, otherwise there is a good chance that if valve bounce occurs the valves will strike the piston.

As well as the cams controlling the points at which the valves open and close, the cams control the amount that the valves open, but simply lifting the valves further is not the answer to improved performance. Greater openings make it more difficult to avoid piston/valve strikes. It is in the design of the points of opening and closing that most benefit will be found, albeit at the expense of noise levels and flexibility. Nor should the shaping of the valve ports themselves be forgotten. The shape of these ducts for incoming gases can help to direct the gas towards the plug and impart a swirl to the incoming gases. Friction caused by poor shaping can slow down the gases in the inlet tract. As the gases are driven out of the cylinder while still at high pressures by the positive compressing affect of the rising piston, exhaust port design is not quite as critical in the early stages of power improvement.

It is most likely then that the developments of model four-stroke engines that will result in power increases will be as a result of multiple detail design improvements. There are not really any radical changes that are likely to be seen. The route towards power improvement by positive induction, whether it be by turbo-charging or supercharging, has not so far shown practical worth in very small engines. Supercharging works by pumping the fuel/air mixture into the combustion chamber instead of relying on the 'suction' of the descending piston to get the mixture into the cylinder, so that it is forced in with the result that much more can be crammed in. Small compressors suffer from poor efficiency and when the amount of power taken actually to drive the compressor or supercharger is considered, the likely result could be an actual reduction of power output.

Using an exhaust-powered turbine to drive the compressor, or in other words turbo-charging, looks a much more practical proposition for model size engines. Some success has already been had with turbo-charging two-strokes of model size, although there is a high penalty in fuel consumption to be paid. It should also be remembered that turbo-charging also increases the effective compression ratio with the attendant problems related to pre-ignition.

Temperature will also play an increasingly dominant part if the super- or turbo-charging route is taken or, it should be said, almost whatever route is taken to increase the power output. After all, we are looking at 'heat engines', and more power means more heat throughput with all the associated problems of both metallurgy and pre-ignition. Although a high percentage of waste heat exhausts through the exhaust port, there is still a fair amount that has to be dissipated through cylinder cooling fins and the crankcase of the engine.

It could well be that the only sure route to dramatic power increases in four-stroke model engines will result in spark ignition replacing glow ignition and water-cooling taking over from air-cooling, a dual-pronged attack on the problems of pre-ignition and overheating.

Although tuned exhaust systems are regularly used to enhance the power output of two-strokes, this means of power boosting is not anything like as practical on the four-stroke. In the first instance the clearing out of the two-stroke cylinder relies on a long overlap of exhaust period and inlet to allow the fresh incoming gases to drive out the burnt residues. The four-stroke inlet valve is theoretically. closed whilst the exhaust is being driven out by the rising piston and, although some overlap is usually designed into the engine this would have to be considerably increased if the principle were to work, giving rise to problems of pollution of incoming charge plus a reduced closed period of the exhaust valve, during which time its contact with the valve seat allows cooling by heat transference. At its best, the four-stroke tuned exhaust is usually reckoned to be simply a means of ensuring that negative pressure waves do not build up to

A Magnum 91 converted to spark ignition by F. Dunham. Addition of contact breaker is main requirement. Some conversions provide one spark per rev. though only one every other rev. is needed.

Fig. 28

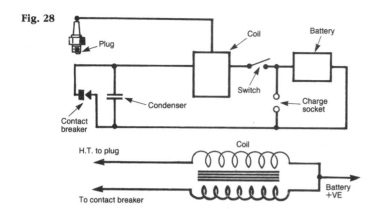

the extent that there is a conflict between them and the outgoing exhaust. This usually means keeping the exhaust system fairly short.

Almost any route towards higher performance implies some form of penalty and I would argue that seeking ever-higher performance in terms of power would be better achieved by larger capacity engines of modest specific output which retain flexibility, reasonable noise levels and the sort of reliability and longevity that accompanies these characteristics.

Spark ignition

Particularly in the field of vintage radio control flying, spark ignition is experiencing a resurgence of popularity. The advantages are particularly apparent with four-strokes, where the precision of ignition timing possible eliminates most of the pre-ignition tendencies associated with glow-plugs. Also, the use of petrol as a fuel cuts running costs and when mixed with mineral oil gives the nostalgic petrol engine smell characteristic of 1940s power flying. Figure 28 shows the standard coil/contact breaker arrangement.

Development of electronic ignition has cut the spark system down to a 'black box' and coil and electro-magnetic sensing has replaced the contact breaker. Advancing and retarding the ignition is also achieved electronically and battery consumption has also dropped noticeably. It is quite a simple matter to fit an electronic spark system to most engines, the only requirement being to fit a small magnet into the propeller driver and mount the sensor close to it. Standard sparking plugs are available that will directly replace the glow-plug and once the system is fixed and running the only other

91

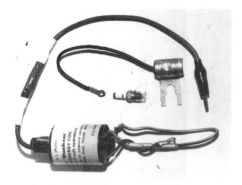

Additional accessories required for spark ignition are coil, condenser and sparking plug plus a battery, which slightly increase airborne weight.

modification to the model will be to replace the usual silicone fuel tubing used with glow fuel for a rubber or neoprene tubing for petrol. It is sometimes necessary to shield the ignition system from the radio receiver and this can be done by placing the coil and other parts in a metal box and then grounding this to the engine crankcase with an earthing strap. The receiver aerial must be routed as far away from the ignition system as possible to avoid ignition interference to the radio. See Figure 29.

As an alternative, a magneto can be used. The magneto is a small direct current generator that incorporates a transformer to boost the output voltage to a sufficiently high level to produce a healthy spark. The magneto has to be positively driven from the crankshaft or cam shaft of the engine, for it is a timed device arranged to generate and transform the current generated once per revolution at precisely the right time for ignition. It does not matter if the magneto is crankshaft driven, for although there will be a spark on the exhaust stroke as well as on the firing stroke if this is done, the engine will not suffer. Incidentally, the Citroen 2CV car engine which uses coil

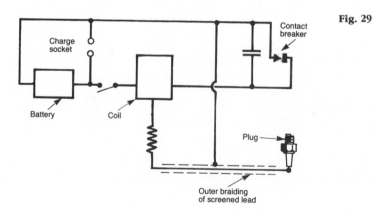

Fig. 29

Fig. 30

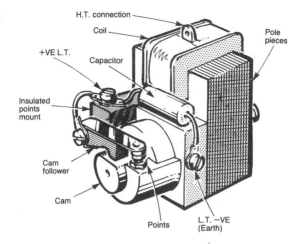

ignition sparks on every revolution. The only detrimental effect is likely to be in bearing and drive train wear if the magneto is running at twice the speed that it need.

Pre-ignition and sparks

Although the ignition point is accurately controlled by spark ignition this does not mean that the possibility of pre-ignition can be

Neat magneto by Gerald Smith, who has a long string of well designed and beautifully built engines to his credit. No additional accessories are needed with a magneto.

93

Display stand shows tidy installation of twin coils and other ignition components on this Kavan 50.

forgotten. Some model four-strokes run at quite high compression ratios and are designed for methanol fuel. Using petrol can lead to pre-ignition which can of course be cured by retarding the ignition point. This will reduce the power output and in extreme cases cause bad overheating, as the fuel can still be burning past the end of the power stroke whereupon the rising piston will be driving still burning gases out of the exhaust port. This is more of a problem with two-strokes where of course the piston will try to compress still burning gases.

Methanol fuel can of course be used with spark ignition, or methanol can be added to the fuel providing that a synthetic or castor oil is being used. As there is really only one type of spark plug available in the size needed for model engines (unless modifications are made to the engine) heat range of the plug is fixed. The heat range can be important, since the plug electrode can tend to glow if the engine becomes overheated, causing once again the dreaded pre-ignition. It should also be remembered that most modern four-strokes are designed for methanol fuels and could run too hot if used with petrol. Anyone attempting to convert a modern four-stroke is advised to proceed with caution, also remembering that modifications carried out on an engine will probably invalidate the manufacturer's guarantee. Nor should the dangers of petrol fuels be forgotten. Carrying petrol in a flight box that contains batteries is absolutely not on: it should be carried in a metal can painted red and clearly marked 'Petrol – Inflammable'. Filling of tanks should be done in such a way as to prevent spillages and the engine should not be started over the point where any spillage has occurred. Even a small spark from a glow battery or starter battery can start a petrol fire and the really wise will carry a small powder fire extinguisher in their flight box as a matter of course.

94

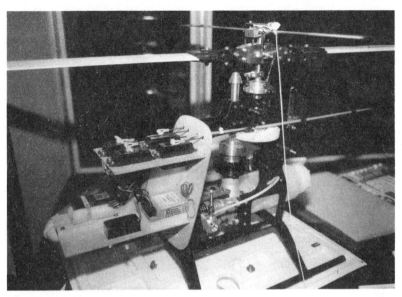

Four-stroke engines in R/C helicopters would have been taken as a joke only four or five years ago. Now their use is growing, as it is in most other spheres of modelling.

In conclusion

Whatever type of four-stroke you choose to buy and operate, be it single or multi-cylinder, rotary valve, poppet valve, home or foreign manufacture, you will surely obtain most satisfaction from it if you use it sensibly within its designed specification and take care to maintain it properly. Engines currently manufactured are produced to a level of quality and performance rarely seen even ten years ago and without exception should give long, reliable and useful service.

The golden rules that govern satisfaction are use the correct sized propeller, never run your engine with too weak a mixture, keep your glow battery fully charged and always clean out your engine after use. The rewards you can expect from a model four-stroke are economy, low noise level, flexibility and high torque at moderate RPM. Do not expect screaming high power but do not be surprised at the flight performance of your model, for the low exhaust noise of a modern four-stroke is very deceptive. Remember that you own a precision piece of engineering and take pleasure in its correct operation.

Appendix 1 – Four-strokes by capacity

An asterisk indicates that no published figure is available.

Engine	Country of origin	Capacity cu.in.	Valve type	Power BHP	RPM	Weight Ounces	Propellers Pitch×Dia	
HP VT-21	Austria	0.211	Rotary	0.24	12,250	11.4	10×4; 9×4,5,6,8; 5×5,6	Vertical axis rotary valve, bevel gear drive, currently smallest capacity production four-stroke
O.S. FS-20	Japan	0.217	OHV	0.3	12,000	9.2	10×4; 9×4,5,6	Reduced size version of OS FS-40, bronze bushed camshaft
HP VT-25	Austria	0.49	Rotary	0.40	15,000	11.30	10×4,5; 9×6	Larger capacity version of earlier VT-21, available in 'buggy' version with heat-sink sylinder head. Peak RPM of buggy motor 23,000, power output 0.45BHP
Saito 30	Japan	0.30	OHV	*	*	11.7	10×4,5,6	Now out of production but still on sale in U.K. at time of publication
Enya 35-4c	Japan	0.35	OHV	0.445	11,000	12.4	10×6; 11×4,5,6	First of the Enya four-strokes, used ABC piston cylinder, now out of production

Left, O.S. FS-90.

Below, the O.S. Max FS-120
and the O.S. Max FS-80.

O.S. 20

97

Engine	Country of origin	Capacity cu.in.	Valve type	Power BHP	RPM	Weight Ounces	Propellers Pitch×Dia	
Enya 40-4c	Japan	0.405	OHV	0.47	11,500	13.0	12×4,5; 11×4,6; 10×6,7	Big bore 35-4c, uses ringed piston, open valve gear. Lowered compression ratio helps cure pre-ignition problems on 35-4c
O.S. FS-40	Japan	0.396	OHV	0.46	11,200	12.0	12×4,5; 11×4,6; 10×6,7	Probably the most popular four-stroke currently available, clean practical design with ball-race mounted crank and cam-shaft
Saito FA-40	Japan	0.402	OHV	0.46	11,300	12.5	12×4,5; 11×4,6; 10×6,7	Now in Mark III version, earlier versions had open valve gear. Chrome plated cylinder
Webra T4-40	West Germany	0.393	Rotary	0.44	12,000	13.4	12×4; 11×4,6; 10×5,6,7	Rotary valve is toothed belt driven on an axis parallel with crankshaft
Laser 45	Britain	0.45	OHV	*	*	15.5	11×6 – 12×6	Engine not in production at the time of going to press
Kalt 45	Japan	0.453	OHV	0.5	10,800	18.5	12×5; 11×5,6	The only four-stroke engine to come from Kalt, now well known for helicopter kit manufacturing
Saito FA-45	Japan	0.457	OHV	0.51	11,400	14.0	14×4; 13×4,5; 12×4,5,6; 11×6	Large bore version of FA-40 fitted with choke flap. Can swing large propellers

O.S. FT-160

SAITO FA-270T

Engine	Country of origin	Capacity cu.in.	Valve type	Power BHP	RPM	Weight Ounces	Propellers Pitch×Dia	
Enya 46-4c	Japan	0.458	OHV	0.72	13,200	14.5	12×4,5,6; 11×5–7; 10×6–8	Much refined development of earlier small capacity Enyas, enclosed valve gear and choke flap. Very high power output for capacity
HP VT-49	Austria	0.49	Rotary	0.73	11,500	22.57	14×4; 12×5,5.5; 11×7; 10×7,8	Second in the line of HP rotary valve four-strokes
RVE 10	Britain	0.607	Rotary	•	9,000	25.0	12×6	Interesting rotary valve design using similar drive system to HP
O.S. FS-60	Japan	0.607	OHV	0.62	10,500	20.8	12×6; 13×5.5	First of the true modern production four-strokes now replaced by FS-61
Enya 60-4c	Japan	0.607	OHV	0.84	11,800	21.9	14×6; 12×6,7; 11×8	Set the design pattern for subsequent Enya four-strokes
HP VT-61	Austria	0.61	Rotary	0.93	12,000	19.60	14×4; 12×5; 11×7; 10×7	Physically the same size as the HP VT-49, latest versions employ a roller thrust race over the rotary valve
O.S. FS-61	Japan	0.607	OHV	0.89	11,500	20.6	15×4; 14×4,5,6; 13×5,6; 12×6,7,8; 11×7½,8	Revised, more powerful version of the original O.S. FS-60, front camshaft and enclosed valve gear

SAITO FA-80T

SAITO 40/45

Engine	Country of origin	Capacity cu.in.	Valve type	Power BHP	RPM	Weight Ounces	Propellers Pitch×Dia	
Webra T4-60	West Germany	0.607	Rotary	0.95	11,000	22.0	11×8	Very simple rotary valve engine with toothed belt drive
Laser 61	Britain	0.606	OHV	1.20	14,040	23.8	11×6,7,8; 12×6; 13×5,6; 14×6	This engine, machined from solid, challenges two-strokes for power output
Saito 65	Japan	0.65	OHV	•	11,500	19.5	10×8; 11×7¾	Latest engine from Saito has brass cylinder liner chrome plated with ringed aluminium piston. Cylinder head is integral with barrel
Laser 75	Britain	0.75	OHV	1.15	12,600	23.8	17×5; 16×5,6; 14×6	Large bore version of the Laser 61, very big increase in torque
Saito FA-80T	Japan	0.803	OHV	•	•	•	•	Horizontally opposed twin, unusual single throw crank design, uneven firing intervals give greater vibration levels but simple construction. Superseded by FA-90T
Enya 80-4c	Japan	0.769	OHV	0.98	11,000	21.2	15×4; 14×4,5,6; 12×7,8	Large bore 60-4c, (+3mm), larger carburettor bore
Saito FA-80	Japan	0.80	OHV	•	11,500	18.0	11×7¾; 13×6; 14×6	Latest of the Saito engines to be released in Japan

HP VT-21

WEBRA T4-60 and 40

Engine	Country of origin	Capacity cu.in.	Valve type	Power BHP	RPM	Weight Ounces	Propellers Pitch×Dia	
Webra T4-80	Austria	0.810	Rotary	1.15	11,000	23.6	14×4,5,6; 13×6; 12×6,7,8	Longitudinal axis rotary valve engine, successor to T4, belt driven valve. Large bore version of T4-60
O.S. FS-80	Japan	0.791	OHV	1.00	11,000	22.0		Physically almost identical to the FS-60 but with a 30 percent increase in capacity
Saito FA-90T	Japan	0.914	OHV	0.93	9,800	28.4	16×4,5,6; 15×4,5,6; 14×6	Horizontally opposed single throw crank twin, uses cylinders of FA-45T single cylinder engine. Crankcase incorporates a unique vane pump helping to prevent gases blowing excess oil past piston
Condor 90	Britain	0.901	Rotary	•	•	•	•	Rotary valve engine that incorporates fuel pump
O.S. FS-90	Japan	0.912	OHV	1.32	11,500	24.4	17×6; 16×4,5,6; 15×4,5,6; 14×6,7,8	Last of the O.S. rear camshaft engines of the O.S. FS-60 line
Magnum 91-S	Britain	0.908	OHV	1.14	9,100	30.8	18×6; 17×6; 16×6; 15×6,7,8; 14×7,8	No longer in production, interesting symmetrical valve timing to allow rotation in either direction
Enya 90-4c	Japan	0.911	OHV	1.28	12,000	29.0	16×4,5,6; 15×6; 14×6,7,8; 13×8,9	Powerful motor for R/C scale

HP VT-49

LASER 61

ENYA 46-4C

105

Engine	Country of origin	Capacity cu.in.	Valve type	Power BHP	RPM	Weight Ounces	Propellers Pitch×Dia	
Webra T4	West Germany	0.873	Rotary	1.10	11,200	36.7	16×4,5; 15×4,5,6; 14×6	Vertical axis Aspin type rotary valve engine now superseded by a Mk II version
Laser 90	Britain	0.90	OHV	•	•	28.0	14×6 – 18×6	Long stroke, high torque engine, can turn at full throttle at as low as 5,000 RPM without protest
Demo 218	Sweden	1.10	OHV	1.19	11,200	24.5	18×5,6; 16×5,6; 14×6	Horizontally opposed twin, the 'No-oil' engine, high quality limited production engine
OPS 120	Italy	1.2	OHC	2.1	12,000	35.5	•	Elegant-looking high performer, overhead camshaft layout first to be seen on a production engine
O.S. Gemini-120	Japan	1.21	OHV	•	10,000	34.1	16×6; 15×4,5,6	Horizontally opposed twin, one of the earlier 'exotic' twins, has proved a reliable practical performer
Enya R120-4c	Japan	1.216	OHV	2.00	12,500	32.6	15×6; 14×8; 13×9	Redesign of 120-4c, higher performance for competition use
O.S. FS-120	Japan	1.218	OHV	1.76	11,000	27.2	18×6; 17×6; 16×6,7,8; 15×6,7,8; 14×7,8,9; 13×9,10	High torque engine, uses multi-bolt propeller fixing

ENYA 90-4C

TECHNOPOWER 9

TECHNOPOWER'S "9"
⅛ Scale
36 C.I.
Glo Ign.
20/6 prop at 6500 rpm

£ 1695.00

This Nine Cyl Radial is
out of stock, but, if we
receive enough orders secured
by a $150.00 deposit we will
do another run of 50 engines
in about 6 months.

$1695.00

107

Engine	Country of origin	Capacity cu.in.	Valve type	Power BHP	RPM	Weight Ounces	Propellers Pitch×Dia	
Condor 120	Britain	1.217	Rotary	•	•	36.7	•	Uncertain future availability for this larger version of Condor 90
Laser 120V 90° Vee Twin	Britain	1.20	OHV	•	•	34.0	14×6 – 18×6	Also available in 1.5 cu.in. version with increased cylinder bore (+0.10in.)
Saito FA-120	Japan	1.217	OHV	•	10,000	32.4	14×8; 15×6	This engine set the trend for subsequent Saito engines by using a fixed cylinder head. Locking propeller nut
Technopower 7 7 Cylinder Radial	USA	1.35	OHV	0.82	8,200	32.2		Superb multi-cylinder motor, early versions suffered from plastic rocker covers, since replaced with die-cast covers
Technopower 5 5 Cylinder Radial	USA	1.39	OHV	0.85	8,200	25.3	17×4,5,6; 16×5,6; 15×6; 14×8	Improved power output from this 5 cylinder engine obtained by increasing capacity
O.S. Gemini-160 Horizontally opposed twin	Japan	1.618	OHV	1.96	10,400	39.4	20×6; 18×6,7,8; 17×6,7,8; 16×6,7,8; 15×7,8,9; 14×8,9,10	Development of the original Gemini, new throughout
Magnum 182-V 90°Vee Twin	Britain	1,817	OHV	•	•	•	•	Uses a pair of Magnum single cylinders, no longer available

ENYA 40, 60 and 90-4C

KAVAN 50

109

Engine	Country of origin	Capacity cu.in.	Valve type	Power BHP	RPM	Weight Ounces	Propellers Pitch×Dia	
O.S. Super Gemini Horizontally opposed twin	Japan	2.44	OHV	3.26	9,000	71.00	22×6,7,8,9,10; 20×8,9,10,11,12; 18×10,11,12	Currently one of the largest four-strokes available, ideal for giant scale
Saito FA-270T Horizontally opposed twin	Japan	2.75	OHV	•	8,000	77.0	22×6,7,8,9,10; 20×8,9,10,12; 18×10,12	This big twin employs a double throw crankshaft supported on three ball-races for smooth running
Kavan 50 Horizontally opposed twin	West Germany	3.00	OHV	4.0	8,800	88.0	22×6,7,8,9,10; 20×8,9,10; 18×10,12	A 'half Continental' even down to the legend on the rocker covers, for giant scale purists
Technopower 9 9 Cylinder Radial	USA	3.6	OHV	•	•	77.0	•	Superb, and the largest capacity model four-stroke available

OPS (PROTOTYPE)

MAGNUM 91

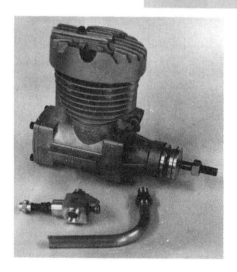

R.V.E. 60

Appendix 2
Major
Engine
Dimensions

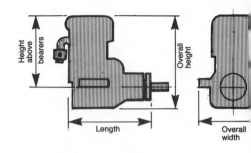

Engine	Overall height	Height above bearers	Overall length to front of prop driver	Overall width
O.S. FS-120	135	114	127	67
O.S. FS-90	121	101	123.5	60
O.S. FS-80	121	102	123	60
O.S. FS-61	120	100	116	58
O.S. FS-40	100	83.3	92	49
O.S. FS-20	84	70	82	43.2
O.S. Gemini 120	85	–	100	200
Saito FA-270T	233	92	175	*
Saito FA-120	132	110	140	69
Saito FA-90T	169	80	100	*
Saito FA-80T	113	93	116	60
Saito FA-65	113	93	115	60
Saito FA-45	102	84	107	54
Saito FA-40	102	84	107	54
H.P. VT-21	83	66	79	49
H.P. VT-49	104	82	100	63
H.P. VT-61	104	82	100	63
Webra T4-40	88	71	82	50
Webra T4-60	107	85	107	60
Webra T4-80	115	94	107	60
Laser 45	100	82	121	54
Laser 61	112	82	130	57
Laser 75	112	82	130	57
Laser 90	122	100	130	62
Laser Vee Twin	*	*	114	*
Enya 46-4c	98	81	100	48
Enya 60-4c	120	99	124	64
Enya 80-4c	120	99	124	64
Enya 90-4c	*	*	*	*
Enya R120-4c	135	112	130	73
Kavan 50	118	*	190	267

Dimensions in mm   * indicates figures not available at publication.